The Four Foundations of Mindfulness in Plain English

The Four Foundations
of Mindfulness
IN PLAIN ENGLISH

Bhante Gunaratana

WISDOM PUBLICATIONS • BOSTON

Wisdom Publications
199 Elm Street
Somerville, MA 02144 USA
www.wisdompubs.org

Library of Congress Cataloging-in-Publication Data

Gunaratana, Henepola, 1927–
The four foundations of mindfulness in plain English / Bhante Gunaratana.
    pages cm
Includes index.
ISBN 1-61429-038-5 (pbk. : alk. paper)
1. Vipasyana (Buddhism) 2. Meditation—Buddhism. I. Title.
BQ5630.V5G857 2013
294.3'4435—dc23

                            2012005119

ISBN 978-1-61429-038-4
eBook ISBN 978-1-61429-042-1

16 15 14 13 12
5 4 3 2 1

Cover and interior design by Gopa&Ted2. Set in Fairfield LT Std Light 11/16.

Wisdom Publications' books are printed on acid-free paper and meet the guidelines for permanence and durability of the Production Guidelines for Book Longevity of the Council on Library Resources.

Printed in the United States of America.

Contents

Preface

THERE ARE several books on the Four Foundations of Mindfulness. Some of them are direct translations of the original Pali discourse of the historical Buddha, some explain the sutta in great detail with commentaries and subcommentaries, some are rich scholarly treatises. And if you are interested in improving your theoretical knowledge of meditation, any of these books can be highly recommended.

When I teach meditation I always try to make sure the listeners can receive the message easily and put it into practice even without a teacher around to consult; as always, my concern in this book is the actual practice, right here in our lives. And when I write, I strive to write everything in plain English.

Meditation is becoming very popular these days for many good reasons. Unfortunately, there are not enough accessible teachers to fully meet the demand of these burgeoning explorers. Some would-be students read good meditation books, some attend meditation retreats, and some listen to many good talks on meditation. After reading books on meditation, listening to talks on meditation, and attending meditation retreats, quite a number of students of meditation write me at the Bhavana Society with questions on matters they would like clarified. I thought of writing this book to answer some, not all, of the questions. Of course, nobody can write one book or series of books answering all the questions people ask! And what's more, as people delve more deeply, their enthusiasm prompts them to ask more questions. The present book is my humble attempt to answer some of the questions related to meditation.

I sincerely thank Ajahn Sona, one of our students at the Bhavana Society, for his valuable help in getting this book started. I am grateful to Josh Bartok and Laura Cunningham at Wisdom Publications for making many valuable suggestions to complete this book and for shepherding it to completion, and to Brenda Rosen who contributed enormous time and effort to develop the manuscript.

Bhante Henepola Gunaratana
Bhavana Society
High View, West Virginia

Introduction

THE FOUR FOUNDATIONS OF MINDFULNESS is a talk or perhaps a collection of talks said to have been given by the historical Buddha. Mindfulness or insight meditation is based on the Four Foundations. Now very well known in the West, this comprehensive set of meditation topics and techniques is probably the preeminent style of meditation taught today in the Theravada Buddhist world.

Mindfulness has also been the focus of my books. In *Mindfulness in Plain English*, I present a practical step-by-step guide to mindfulness meditation. If you are new to insight practice, this book is a good place to start. In *Eight Mindful Steps to Happiness*, I show how mindfulness is used to progress along the Buddha's eight-step path to happiness. You could say that the Four Foundations are the details of the seventh step of the Buddha's path. In fact, the last three steps—effort, mindfulness, and concentration, which we in the West call "meditation"— are all covered in the Four Foundations. In *Beyond Mindfulness in Plain English*, I explain the principles and techniques of deep concentration meditation. Concentration meditation or *samatha* is parallel and complementary to mindfulness meditation or *vipassana*, since the Four Foundations are the basis of all concentration.

Now, in this book, I write directly about the Four Foundations, the underlying principles of mindfulness practice. In simple and straightforward language, I share what the Buddha said about mindfulness in his instructional talks or *suttas* and how we can use these principles to improve our daily lives, deepen our mindfulness, and move closer to our spiritual goals.

The basic premise of mindfulness is simple. The body does many things without our awareness. When germs invade, our white blood cells attack the invaders without our knowledge. However, we can train ourselves to become aware of the things we do consciously with the body, such as walking, standing, talking, eating, drinking, writing, reading, playing, and other physical activities. We can also develop moment-to-moment awareness of our emotions, sensations, thoughts, and other mental activities. *Mindfulness trains us to do everything we do with full awareness.*

You may be wondering, "Why is full awareness important?" As anyone who tries mindfulness practice quickly discovers, the more aware we are of our actions and of the feelings, thoughts, and perceptions that give rise to them, the more insight we have into why we are doing what we are doing. Awareness allows us to see whether our actions spring from beneficial or harmful impulses. Beneficial motivations include generosity, friendliness, compassion, and wisdom; harmful actions are caused primarily by greed, hatred, and delusion. When we are mindful of the deep roots from which our thoughts, words, and deeds grow, we have the opportunity to cultivate those that are beneficial and weed out those that are harmful.

The Buddha is very clear that the primary aim of all his teachings is "the end of suffering." Mindfulness helps us to recognize that beneficial actions bring peace of mind and happiness to our everyday lives. They also help us progress on the Buddha's path toward *nibbana*—liberation, complete freedom from suffering. Similarly, mindfulness teaches us that actions motivated by greed, hatred, and delusion make us miserable and anxious. They imprison us in *samsara*, the life-after-life cycle of repeated suffering.

When we practice mindfulness, before we speak we ask ourselves: "Are these words truthful and beneficial to me and to others? Will they bring peace, or will they create problems?" When we think mindfully, we ask: "Does this thought make me calm and happy, or distressed and fearful?" Before we act, we ask: "Will this action cause suffering for me and for others?" Being mindful gives us the opportunity to choose: "Do I want joy and contentment or misery and worry?"

Mindfulness also trains us to remember to pay attention to the changes that are continually taking place inside our body and mind and in the world around us. Normally, we forget to pay attention because the countless things that are happening simultaneously distract our minds. We get carried away by the superficial and lose sight of the flow. The mind wants to see what is next, what is next, and what is next. We get excited by the show and forget that it is, indeed, simply a show.

The Buddha taught: "That which is impermanent is suffering." The truth of these words becomes clear when we simply pay attention. Eventually, the mind gets tired of moving from one impermanent thing to the next. Losing interest in the futile pursuit, the mind rests and finds joy. In Pali, the word for "to remember" is *sati*, which can also be translated as "mindfulness." Remembering is simply paying direct, non-verbal attention to what is happening from one moment to the next.

Resting comfortably in awareness, we relax into things as they are right now in this very moment, without slipping away into what happened in the past or will happen in the future. Normally, because we do not understand, we tend to blame the world for our pain and suffering. But with sati, mindful remembering, we understand that the only place to find peace and freedom from suffering is this very place, right here in our own body and mind.

Memory is very natural to our body, almost automatic. Our hearts pump blood without our reminding them to do so. The mind can also be taught to act the same way. Training the faculty of mindfulness is like breathing oxygen continuously to remain alive. As mental events occur, mindfulness helps us see whether they hurt our mind and body. We have the choice: Do we merely suffer from pain, or do we examine the pain to understand why it arises? If we ignore the causes, we continue to suffer. Living with awareness requires effort, but following the Buddha's example, with practice anyone can master it.

Mindfulness practice has deep roots in Buddhist tradition. More than 2,600 years ago, the Buddha exhorted his senior *bhikkhus*, monks with the responsibility of passing his teachings on to others, to train their students in the Four Foundations of Mindfulness.

"What four?" he was asked.

"Come, friends," the Buddha answered. "Dwell contemplating the body in the body, ardent, clearly comprehending, unified, with concentrated one-pointed mind, in order to know the body as it really is. Dwell contemplating feeling in feelings . . . in order to know feelings as they really are. Dwell contemplating mind in mind . . . in order to know mind as it really is. Dwell contemplating dhamma in dhammas . . . in order to know dhammas as they really are."

The practice of contemplating (or as we might say, meditating on) the Four Foundations—mindfulness of the body, feelings, mind, and dhammas (or phenomena)—is recommended for people at every stage of the spiritual path. As the Buddha goes on to explain, everyone— trainees who have recently become interested in the Buddhist path, monks and nuns, and even *arahants*, advanced meditators who have already reached the goal of liberation from suffering, "should be exhorted, settled, and established in the development of these Four Foundations of Mindfulness."

In this sutta, the Buddha is primarily addressing the community of bhikkhus, monks and nuns who have dedicated their lives to spiritual practice. Given this, you might wonder whether people with families and jobs and busy Western lives can benefit from mindfulness practice. If the Buddha's words were meant only for monastics, he would have given this talk in a monastery. But he spoke in a village filled with shopkeepers, farmers, and other ordinary folk. Since mindfulness can help men and women from all walks of life relieve suffering, we can assume that the word "bhikkhu" is used to mean anyone seriously interested in meditation. In that sense, we are all bhikkhus.

Let's look briefly at each of the Four Foundations of Mindfulness as a preview of things to come.

By asking us to practice *mindfulness of the body*, the Buddha is reminding us to see "the body in the body." By these words he means that we should recognize that the body is not a solid unified thing, but rather a collection of parts. The nails, teeth, skin, bones, heart, lungs, and all other parts—each is actually a small "body" that is located *in* the larger entity that we call "the body." Traditionally, the human body is divided into thirty-two parts, and we train ourselves to be mindful of each. Trying to be mindful of the entire body is like trying to grab a heap of oranges. If we grab the whole heap at once, perhaps we will end up with nothing!

Moreover, remembering that the body is composed of many parts helps us to see "the body as body"—not as *my* body or as *myself*, but simply as a physical form like all other physical forms. Like all forms, the body comes into being, remains present for a time, and then passes away. Since it experiences injury, illness, and death, the body is unsatisfactory as a source of lasting happiness. Since it is not *myself*, the body can also be called "selfless." When mindfulness helps us to recognize that the body is impermanent, unsatisfactory, and selfless, in the Buddha's words, we "know the body as it really is."

Similarly, by asking us to practice *mindfulness of feelings*, the Buddha is telling us to contemplate "the feeling in the feelings." These words remind us that, like the body, feelings can be subdivided. Traditionally, there are only three types—pleasant feelings, unpleasant feelings, and neutral feelings. Each type is one "feeling" *in* the mental awareness that we call "feelings." At any given moment we are able to notice only one type. When a pleasant feeling is present, neither a painful feeling nor a neutral feeling is present. The same is true of an unpleasant or neutral feeling.

We regard feelings in this way to help us develop a simple non-judgmental awareness of what we are experiencing—seeing a particular feeling as one of many feelings, rather than as *my* feeling or as part of *me*. As we watch each emotion or sensation as it arises, remains present, and passes away, we observe that any feeling is impermanent. Since a pleasant feeling does not last and an unpleasant feeling is often painful, we understand that feelings are unsatisfactory. Seeing a feeling as an emotion or sensation rather than as *my* feeling, we come to know that feelings are selfless. Recognizing these truths, we "know feelings as they really are."

The same process applies to *mindfulness of mind*. Although we talk about "the mind" as if it were a single thing, actually, mind or consciousness is a succession of particular instances of "mind *in* mind." As mindfulness practice teaches us, consciousness arises from moment to moment on the basis of information coming to us from the senses—what we see, hear, smell, taste, and touch—and from internal mental states, such as memories, imaginings, and daydreams. When we look at the mind, we are not looking at mere consciousness. The mind alone cannot exist, only particular states of mind that appear depending on external or internal conditions. Paying attention to the way each thought arises, remains present, and passes away, we learn to stop the runaway train of one unsatisfactory thought leading to another and another and another. We gain a bit of detachment and understand that we are not our thoughts. In the end, we come to know "mind as it really is."

By telling us to practice *mindfulness of dhammas*, or phenomena, the Buddha is not simply saying that we should be mindful of his teachings, though that is one meaning of the word "dhamma." He is also reminding us that the dhamma that we contemplate is within us. The history of the world is full of truth seekers. The Buddha was one of them. Almost all sought the truth outside themselves. Before he attained enlightenment, the Buddha also searched outside of himself. He was looking for his maker, the cause of his existence, who he called the "builder of this house." But he never found what he was looking for. Instead, he discovered that he himself was subject to birth, growth, decay, death, sickness, sorrow, lamentation, and defilement. When he looked outside himself, he saw that everyone else was suffering from these same problems. This recognition helped him to see that no one outside himself could free him from his suffering. So he began to search within. This inner seeking is known as "come and see." Only when he began to search inside did he find the answer. Then he said:

> Many a birth I wandered in samsara,
> Seeking but not finding the builder of this house.
> Sorrowful is it to be born again and again.
> Oh! House builder thou art seen.
> Thou shall not build house again.
> All thy rafters are broken.
> Thy ridgepole is shattered.
> The mind has attained the unconditioned.

The great discovery of the Buddha is that the truth is within us. The entire Dhamma that he taught is based on this realization. When we look inside, we come to understand the significance of the Four Noble Truths—the Buddha's essential first teaching. Where do we find suffering? We experience it within ourselves. And where is the cause of our suffering, craving? It, too, is within us. And, how can we reach the end of it, the cessation of suffering? We find the way within ourselves. And where do we develop skillful understanding, thinking, speech, action, livelihood, effort, mindfulness, and concentration, the Buddha's Noble Eightfold Path—the method for ending suffering? We develop all of these qualities within our own body and mind. The roots of suffering are within us. And the method for eliminating suffering is within us as well.

When we practice mindfulness, we follow the Buddha's example and look inside. We become aware that our own greed, hatred, and delusion are the causes of our unhappiness. When we replace these poisons with generosity, loving-friendliness, compassion, appreciative joy, patience, cordiality, gentleness, and wisdom, we find the happiness and peace of mind we have been seeking. As I always remind my students, "The meditation you do on the cushion is your homework. The rest of your life is your fieldwork. To practice mindfulness, you need both."

The other meaning of *dhammas* is simply "phenomena." When we follow the Buddha's advice and "dwell contemplating dhamma in dhammas," we come to understand that each individual phenomenon within reality as we experience it, including physical objects, feelings, perceptions, mental activities, and consciousness, comes into being, remains, and then passes away. In the same way, the deep-rooted negative habits of the unenlightened mind that bind us to one unsatisfactory life after another, known as the fetters, are impermanent. With effort, each fetter—including greed, hatred, and belief in the existence of a permanent self or soul—can be recognized and removed. In essence, the dhamma path is quite straightforward. We eliminate our harmful habits one by one and cultivate beneficial qualities based on our understanding of each of the Buddha's teachings. In the end, the last fetter falls away, and we achieve liberation from suffering.

So how do we get started with mindfulness meditation? I always recommend meditation focused on the breath as the best way to begin mindfulness training. In *Mindfulness in Plain English*, I explain the basics of breath meditation and other essential mindfulness practices. Similar instructions for sitting meditation and walking meditation can be found in this book in the chapters on mindfulness of the body. In the section that follows this introduction, I suggest ways to include the Buddha's Four Foundations of Mindfulness Sutta in a simple daily practice.

While many people are drawn to meditation because of its wonderful benefits for relaxation, relief from stress and pain, and the general health of the body and mind, in the context of the Four Foundations, it's important to keep another set of goals in mind. With dedicated effort and regular practice, we can look forward to five significant spiritual accomplishments:

First, meditation helps us become fully aware of what is going on in the mind and body here and now. All too often, we sleepwalk through our days, musing about the past or daydreaming about the future. Mindfulness teaches us to cut through the fog and bring our focus to the present moment.

Second, because of this new awareness, we are able to evaluate more clearly the purpose and suitability of everything we say and do. As a result, we make wiser and more beneficial choices.

Third, meditation trains us to see our own body, feelings, perceptions, thoughts, and consciousness exactly as they are, from moment to moment. Seeing ourselves clearly is the essential first step to making positive life changes.

Fourth, as our practice deepens, we see the world around us in a special way, without distortion. We come to understand that everything that exists—including us—is interdependent with everything else, and that everything is always changing. For this reason, we realize, no person, place, thing, or situation can ever be permanently satisfying.

And finally, we learn to dedicate ourselves fully to reflection or meditation, recognizing that only by following the Buddha's example can we hope to find lasting happiness and peace.

In a nutshell, insight meditation trains the mind to be aware twenty-four hours a day. With this new clarity, we begin to perceive material objects as less solid than our ordinary senses tell us they are. In fact, we discover, they are only as real as a mirage shimmering in the desert. In the same way, we recognize that our thoughts and feelings are always in flux. In truth, they are only as permanent as soap bubbles. Awareness frees us from the desire to grasp on to things and other people with the thought "this is *mine*" and to view our own body and mind as fixed and unchanging with the thought "this *I* am" or "this is my *self*."

The Four Foundations of Mindfulness is a powerful teaching. In fact, the Buddha promises that anyone who practices his mindfulness instructions, exactly as they are given, without leaving anything out, can attain enlightenment—permanent liberation from suffering—in this very life, even in as short a time as seven days!

Amazing as that guarantee sounds, it makes perfect sense. Imagine how clear your mind would be if you were mindful during every waking moment for just one day from morning to evening. Then imagine how clear it would be if you spent two days with mindfulness, three days, four days. When we remain mindful all the time, it's easy to make good choices. The mind is purified and becomes luminous. Every day that we practice mindfulness moves us closer to liberation.

The Four Foundations of Mindfulness Sutta

BEFORE WE TURN to a detailed consideration of each of the Four Foundations, let's look ahead to what we will be covering. As I mentioned, the teachings on the Four Foundations come down to us from a teaching talk given by the Buddha known as the Satipatthana Sutta. A summarized version of the sutta is given below. I have added headings not part of the original sutta to help you follow the sequence.

As you read this book, you may find it helpful to turn back to it from time to time to refresh your memory about what's been covered and look ahead at what's to come. Try reading the sutta out loud when you turn to it. It's beneficial to hear the Buddha's words as if they were intended specifically for you—which, of course, they are!

A word of advice: This book is not meant to be read like a novel or digested like a university textbook. Rather, the teachings of the Buddha are to be explored and practiced, more like a piece of great music. As your familiarity grows, your experiential understanding of the Dhamma takes on a life of its own. In the beginning, mindfulness takes much effort, but eventually, it becomes second nature.

A DAILY MINDFULNESS PRACTICE

If you're already practicing meditation, or if reading this book inspires you to start, you can make reading the Satipatthana Sutta part of your meditation session.

I always recommend that people begin a session of meditation with thoughts of loving-friendliness for their parents, teachers, relatives, friends, strangers, adversaries, and ultimately, for all living beings. Starting your meditation session in this way helps develop your concentration and also avoid any resentment that may arise as you sit.

Then, before turning your attention to the breath or other point of focus, you may find it worthwhile to read aloud, recite, or even chant the version of the Satipatthana Sutta given below. Read or recite slowly, to give yourself time to review in your mind what you've learned or understood about each point. If you find that you cannot remember the Buddha's meaning or that you are confused about something, resolve to read more or to ask a more experienced meditator for help. If you read and think about the sutta every day, eventually the whole sequence of mindfulness practices will be at the tip of your tongue.

THE FOUR FOUNDATIONS OF MINDFULNESS SATIPATTHANA SUTTA

Bhikkhus, this is the direct path for the purification of beings,
for the surmounting of sorrow and lamentation,
for the disappearance of pain and grief,
for the attainment of the true way,
for the realization of nibbana—namely,
the Four Foundations of Mindfulness.

1. *Mindfulness of the Body*
Mindfulness of the breath.
Mindfulness of the four postures: walking, standing, sitting, and lying down.
Mindfulness with clear comprehension: of what is beneficial, of suitability, of the meditator's domain, of non-delusion.

Reflection on the thirty-two parts of the body.
Analysis of the four elements.
Nine cemetery contemplations.

2. *Mindfulness of Feelings*
Pleasant, painful, and neither-painful-nor-pleasant feelings,
worldly and spiritual.
Awareness of their manifestation, arising, and disappearance.

3. *Mindfulness of Mind*
Understanding the mind as:
greedy or not greedy,
hateful or not hateful,
deluded or not deluded,
contracted or distracted,
not developed or developed,
not supreme or supreme,
not concentrated or concentrated,
not liberated or liberated.
Awareness of its manifestation, arising, and disappearance.

4. *Mindfulness of Dhamma*
FIVE MENTAL HINDRANCES
Sense desire, ill will, sloth and torpor,
restlessness and worry, skeptical doubt.
Awareness of their manifestation, origin, and disappearance.

FIVE AGGREGATES OF CLINGING
Material form, feelings, perceptions,
mental formations, and consciousness.
Awareness of their manifestation, arising, and dissolution.

SIX INTERNAL AND SIX EXTERNAL SENSE BASES

Eye and visible objects, ear and sounds, nose and smells, tongue
and tastes, body and tangible objects, mind and mental objects.
Knowledge of them, and of the arising, abandoning, and
future non-arising of the fetters that originate dependent on both.

SEVEN FACTORS OF ENLIGHTENMENT

Mindfulness, investigation of Dhamma, energy,
joy, tranquility, concentration, and equanimity.
Knowledge of their presence, their arising, and their development.

FOUR NOBLE TRUTHS

Suffering, its origin, its cessation,
and the path that leads to the cessation of suffering.

NOBLE EIGHTFOLD PATH

Skillful understanding, thinking, speech, action, livelihood,
effort, mindfulness, and concentration.

Bhikkhus, if anyone should properly develop these Four Foundations
of Mindfulness for seven years . . . or even for seven days,
one of two fruits could be expected for that person:
either final knowledge here and now,
or, if there is a trace of clinging left, the state of non-returning.

PART I:

Mindfulness of the Body

1: *Breath*

Twenty years after the Buddha attained enlightenment, a senior monk by the name of Ananda became his personal attendant. One day he asked the Buddha, "Venerable sir, if people ask me whether you are still practicing meditation, what shall I tell them?"

The Buddha replied that, yes, he was still meditating.

"What kind of meditation do you practice, venerable sir?" Ananda asked.

"Mindfulness of breathing," the Buddha answered.

Meditation on the breath is the ideal way to get started with mindfulness training. Breathing is our most constantly repeated physical action. The mind can always return to the breath as an object of focus because it is always with us. We don't need to be taught to breathe. Nor do we need long experience with meditation to place our attention on the breath. The breath is also our life force. No organ in the body can function without the supply of oxygen we get from the cycle of breathing in and breathing out.

Moreover, breathing is not exclusive. Living beings differ in appearance and behavior. They eat various kinds of food. They sleep in many types of beds. But all living beings breathe. Breathing does not differentiate among Buddhists, Christians, Hindus, Sikhs, Jews, Muslims, and Zoroastrians. Nor does it distinguish between rich and poor, capitalists and socialists, or conservatives and liberals, for that matter. When we focus on the breath, we become mindful of the universal nature of all beings.

Although we have been breathing our entire life, until we pay attention to the process, we do not know what is really happening. But when we focus the mind on the breath, we discover everything related to the breath. Training in this way is so essential to our peace of mind and spiritual progress that the Buddha recommends that everyone practice meditation on the breath.

Even the Buddha used mindfulness of breathing to achieve his goal. After his enlightenment, the Buddha described how he had previously practiced extreme self-discipline by manipulating his breath in arcane and special ways. But he discovered that he could not get rid of impurities by holding his breath or altering his breathing. So he gave up breath-control exercises and followed his own middle way.

In the gathering dusk, on the night he would attain enlightenment, the Buddha asked himself, "What subject of meditation should I practice?" Then he remembered. "Ah! When I was a child, I used the breath. Let me use the breath again." So he focused his mind on the breath, just as it was. After long hours of unwavering mindfulness and deep concentration, everything became clear to him. The last of his negative mental habits disappeared, and he reached enlightenment—full and complete liberation from suffering.

THE BUDDHA'S INSTRUCTIONS

In one of the most important suttas, the Buddha explains in detail how to practice mindfulness of breathing. He suggests that people go to a quiet place, such as a forest or a house with few noises—somewhere they have undisturbed solitude and can withdraw from everyday concerns. There, he says, begin by establishing mindfulness "in front."

By these words he doesn't mean that we should place our attention on what is in front of us in space. Rather, we focus on the present moment. We cannot live in the past, nor can we live in the future. Even when we remember something that happened in the past, we understand that this memory is occurring now. The only place and time truly available to us is right here and right now. For this reason, we establish mindfulness by paying attention to this very instance of breathing in and breathing out.

Having established the mind in the present moment, the Buddha continues, sit in a comfortable posture, with the body straight—upright but not uptight. I explain more fully about comfortable postures for sitting meditation in the next chapter. Then focus the mind on the breath, going in and going out, in and out.

Among other things, we become aware that sometimes the breath is long and sometimes short. These variations are natural. If we watch a baby sleeping, we observe that the baby breathes for a while in a regular rhythm. Then she takes a long breath. Then she goes back to her previous rhythm.

As the Buddha explains, when we breathe in long, we understand, "I breathe in long," and when we breathe out long, we understand, "I breathe out long." Breathing in short, we understand, "I breathe in short." Breathing out short, we understand, "I breathe out short." This advice can be misinterpreted to mean that we should force ourselves to take long inhaling breaths and long exhaling breaths, or short inhaling breaths and short exhaling breaths. But when we deliberately alter the duration, our breathing does not follow its natural rhythm. Soon, we get tired. Meditation on the breath is not a breathing exercise. We are simply using the breath as a point of focus to cultivate mindfulness.

As we discover, when we pay attention to its natural rhythm, the breath becomes calm. Simultaneously, the mind quiets down. It all happens naturally. Mindfulness itself makes the breath relax. Any force is counterproductive. Agitation or extra effort makes our breathing speed up. When this happens, we pay attention to the fast breathing and notice the agitation. Then we relax the mind, and the agitation disappears by itself.

We also notice that when we inhale and exhale with mindfulness, we experience the feeling of each breath. The sensations change as the breath changes. So we observe the changing breath and the changing sensations. We find, for instance, that sometimes the breath is shallow; other times it is deep. Sometimes it is easy to breathe; other times, not so easy. We watch these variations.

Along with this, we notice another pattern of subtle feelings, a little bit of anxiety and relief of anxiety, pressure and release of pressure, for instance. Mindfulness helps us notice that when the lungs are full of air, we feel a slight pressure or tension in our lungs. As we breathe out, this tension is slowly released. But when there is no more air in our lungs, we experience a degree of anxiety because there is no air in our lungs. So we breathe in again, and this anxiety fades away. As it does, we experience a degree of pleasure but also the return of pressure.

Of course, we have to pay total attention to the cycle of breathing to notice these changes. We soon discover that there is no escape from them. We inhale and experience pleasure and then tension. We exhale and experience release but also anxiety. But even this pattern has much to teach us. When we experience tension, we remind ourselves not to be disappointed. When we experience pleasure, we remember not to attach to it.

So, as we breathe in and out, we strive to maintain equanimity, a balanced mind. We remind ourselves that our underlying preference for pleasant feelings often arises from desire, which can lead to greed for sensual pleasure. But when we crave pleasure, we always end up suffering, because like all impermanent things, pleasure eventually changes or disappears. We also remember that our underlying tendency to avoid unpleasant feelings often arises from resentment, which can lead to anger. We observe these tendencies, our greed and our anger, and then let them go, returning our attention to the breath.

The Breath-Body

We also pay attention to how we feel at the beginning, the middle, and the end of each in-breath and out-breath. This awareness of the entire breathing cycle is called mindfulness of the breath-body. While the mind is engaged with the breath-body, the mind and the breath are relaxed. When they are relaxed, the rest of our body is also relaxed. This is so because the breath is part of the body. Paying attention to the breath-body is an aspect of being mindful of "the body in the body," as the Buddha recommends. Mindfulness helps us see that the breath and the body are not completely separate.

We experience the relationship between breath and body when we notice the rising and falling of the abdomen during the breathing cycle, as some meditation teachers suggest. When we breathe in, the abdomen expands, and when we breathe out, it contracts. But actually, the movement of the abdomen is the second stage of the body's rising and falling. The first stage occurs at the tip of the nose. Inhaling is rising and exhaling is falling. With mindfulness, we notice in a microscopic way our body's expansion or rising as we breathe in and contraction or falling as we breathe out.

While noticing these events, we also feel expansion, contraction, and other subtle movements in the entire body. These same motions occur in every material object. Even walls breathe! In summer, they expand; in winter, they contract. Astrophysicists tell us that the whole universe is actually expanding and contracting. To practice mindfulness of breathing, however, we need awareness only of the expansion and contraction in our own body.

Internal and External Elements

Another way we become aware of the relationship between the breath and the body is by noting that the breath is made up of four elements—

earth, water, air, and heat. All material objects, including the body, are composed of these elements.

As we practice mindfulness of breathing, we recognize that it is the breath's earth element—its form or shape—that gives rise to pressure, release, and other sensations of touch in the nose, lungs, and abdomen. Similarly, we notice that the breath is dry when its water element is low. When we are aware of moisture in the breath, its water element is high.

The function of the air element is motion and energy. We experience the movement of the breath because of its air element. The temperature of the breath is due to its heat element. Heat fluctuates. When its heat element is high, we call the breath hot. When it goes down, we call the breath cold.

In addition to the four elements, the parts of the body—including the breath—are described as internal or external. The elements inside the body are internal; those outside are external. If we think about this distinction, it may occur to us that the breath that we have inhaled is internal. When we exhale, this internal breath mixes with the external air. Then the breath is external. We might also say that the internal body is inhaling, and the external body is exhaling.

In the Maha Rahulovada Sutta, the Buddha explains the meaning of the words "internal" and "external" as they apply to the four elements of the body. In terms of the air element, he says, "Whatever internally, belonging to oneself, is air . . . that is up-going winds, down-going winds, winds in limbs, in-breath and out-breath . . . this is called the internal air element."

Moreover, the Buddha explains, "Both the internal air element and the external air element are simply air element." This point is important because of our tendency to cling to things we perceive as belonging to us. But seen with "proper wisdom," we recognize that even the air we inhale—the internal air—"is not mine, this I am not, and this is not my self. When one sees it thus as it actually is . . . one becomes disenchanted with the air element and makes the mind dispassionate toward the air element."

Further, the Buddha continues, from time to time, the external air element is disturbed. It "sweeps away villages, towns, cities, districts, and countries," as it does in a hurricane or tornado. At other times, such as during the last month of the hot season, people "seek wind by means of a fan or bellows, and even the stands of straw in the drip-fringe of the thatch do not stir."

These seasonal changes in the external air, which we have all experienced, demonstrate vividly that the air element, "great as it is, is seen to be impermanent, subject to destruction, disappearance, and change." The same applies to the earth, water, and heat elements inside the body and outside the body. Since this is so, the Buddha asks, "what of this body, which is clung to by craving and lasts but a while?" Our body, too, he reminds us, is composed of four elements, which are always being destroyed, disappearing, or changing. Therefore, he concludes, "There can be no considering that as *I* or *mine* or *I am*."

BREATH AND THE AGGREGATES

As we see from our discussion of the four elements of the breath, mindfulness of breathing is instructive in many important ways. If we follow the Buddha's example and use the breath to examine our mind-body system as it is, we gain insight into a number of essential Dhamma points. As the Buddha explains, "All dhammas arise from attention." Among these, we gain firsthand knowledge of the five aggregates—form, feeling, perception, thought, and consciousness—the traditional constituents of the body and mind.

Let's look briefly at the five aggregates as they apply to the breath. The breath-body and all other material objects including the physical body belong to the *aggregate of form*. We have already noted that we experience the touch of the breath at the nose, lungs, and abdomen because the breath has a kind of form or shape. From moment to moment, the form of the breath changes, as we can see when we focus our attention at the nose or abdomen.

The other four aggregates describe our mental experience. The *aggregate of feeling* refers to our sensations of the breath and the emotions we experience as a result. The anxiety we feel when we sense that our lungs are empty and our feeling of relief when we inhale belong to this aggregate. Next is the *aggregate of perception*. We can use the breath as an object of meditation only because our minds perceive it.

The *aggregate of thought* includes all other mental activities, including ideas, opinions, and decisions. The thought "this is the feeling of the breath" and the decision to pay attention to the breath belong to this aggregate. The last of the five, the *aggregate of consciousness*, is the basis of all mental experience. We become aware of changes in the other four aggregates because of the aggregate of consciousness. But consciousness, too, is changing as the form of the breath and our feelings, perceptions, and thoughts change.

In the sutta on mindfulness of breathing, the Buddha tells us: "Mindful of impermanence breathe in, mindful of impermanence breathe out; mindful of dispassion breathe in, mindful of dispassion breathe out; mindful of cessation breathe in, mindful of cessation breathe out; mindful of relinquishing breathe in, mindful of relinquishing breathe out."

When we apply these words to the aggregates of the breath, we notice that all five consist of three very minor moments: the rising moment, the living or enduring moment, and the passing away moment. The same is true of all things that exist. This activity never stops. Such is the nature of impermanence. Forms, feelings, perceptions, thoughts, and even consciousness itself don't stick around. They cease without leaving a trace. Once they are gone, they are gone forever. New forms, feelings, perceptions, thoughts, and consciousness always appear. Observing these changes teaches us detachment and makes it easier for us to relinquish the habit of clinging to any part of the body or mind.

Patience and Joy

Below I suggest a basic technique for getting started with mindfulness meditation on the breath. Take time to work with the practice. Try not to be impatient or rush ahead to experience something new. Allow things to unfold naturally.

People these days are good at making things happen very quickly. Computers, email, and mobile telephones are fast. Washers and dryers, instant breadmaking machines, and instant coffeemakers are time-savers. But too many people don't have time to smile. They don't have time to allow joy to develop the natural way.

One day, a man who wanted to take my picture asked me to relax and be natural. When his camera was ready, he said, "Bhante, smile."

So I said to him, "First you ask me to be natural. Now you are asking me to smile. Do you want me to smile or be natural?"

When something is funny, smiling happens naturally. We also smile when our stress, tension, and fear disappear. Then our face becomes calm and peaceful, and we smile with our hearts without showing our teeth. That is the kind of smile the Buddha had all the time.

As we gain experience with mindfulness of breathing, we gradually overcome sleepiness, restlessness, and other obstacles to concentration. As our concentration deepens, we begin to smile with our hearts. It's not hard to understand why this happens. As we have seen, the breath is part of the body. When we relax the breath, the body becomes relaxed. The breath is free from greed, hatred, delusion, and fear. When the mind joins with the breath, the mind temporarily becomes free from greed, hatred, delusion, and fear. Relaxing the breath, breathe in. Relaxing the breath, breathe out. Then joy arises naturally.

With every small step of meditation, you gain a small degree of insight. Do your practice with patience. Don't rush. Let the insights unfold. Consider the analogy of an impatient hen who lays a few eggs. She wants to see chicks coming out of them quickly, so she turns them over very often to check. But she will never see chicks coming out of these eggs. Another hen lays a few eggs and sits on them patiently. When the eggs are properly hatched, the chicks break the eggshells with their little claws and bills. Then this mother hen sees good feathery results!

KEY POINTS FOR MEDITATION ON THE BREATH

▸ Go to a quiet place where you will be alone and not disturbed.

▸ Bring your attention to the present moment.

▸ Sit in a comfortable posture that allows your upper body to be straight and relaxed, upright but not uptight.

▸ Place your hands on the lap, palms upward, with the right hand on top of the left and the thumbs touching at the tips.

▸ Close your eyes or leave them half-open.

▸ Focus your attention on the breath, coming in and going out.

▸ To deepen your mindfulness, try counting:

   Inhale and exhale. Say silently "one."

   Inhale and exhale. Say silently "two."

   Inhale and exhale. Say silently "three."

   Continue up to ten.

   Inhale and exhale. Say silently "ten."

   Inhale and exhale. Say silently "nine."

   Inhale and exhale. Say silently "eight."

   Continue down to one.

- When you complete this round of counting, settle on your primary object—breath, feeling, thought, rising and falling, or consciousness.

- If restlessness, agitation, or doubt occurs, don't intensify the distraction by following it. Instead, say to your self, "Let me think how I started. I started from my breath. It is not difficult to find my breath." Breathe several times quickly and return your attention to the breath and its natural pace.

- If your mind wanders from its focus on the breath, don't get upset. Simply noticing that you have been thinking, daydreaming, or worrying is a wonderful achievement! Gently but firmly return your attention to the breath. And then do it again the next time, and the next time, and the time after that.

- If you feel sleepy or dull, try focusing with slightly more effort on the touch sensations of the in-breath and out-breath. If stronger focus does not help, stand up and continue meditating in a standing posture for a few minutes or try walking meditation. You'll find instructions for both postures in the next chapter.

- If you begin to feel pain, first try to address the situation as much as possible. Loosen your clothing and check your posture to make sure that you are not slouching. Move to a posture that's easier to maintain (as described in the next chapter). If these adjustments do not help, then work with the pain: try making the sensation of pain your object of meditation. Observe the sensation and watch how it changes over time.

- If questions arise, ask someone with more experience. Remind yourself that millions of people have used this practice to attain clarity and peace of mind.

- Keep practicing with patience.

2: *Four Postures*

For one entire night, Venerable Ananda practiced the Four Foundations of Mindfulness. Because his mindfulness was pure, sharp, and powerful, he perceived that each part of his body, each tiny physical movement, feeling, perception, thought, and even consciousness itself is impermanent, unsatisfactory, and selfless.

At dawn, as he was beginning to lie down, he lifted his foot. In that instant, he reached enlightenment.

Certainly, when the mind is perfectly clear and mindfulness is strong, it is possible to attain enlightenment quickly, even while lifting a foot.

WE CAN DEVELOP mindfulness by paying complete attention to any part of the body. We have already seen how mindfulness of breathing helps us become more calm and peaceful and gain valuable insights into the Buddha's message. The same applies to focusing on the body's positions and movements.

In the sutta on the Four Foundations of Mindfulness, the Buddha explains how mindfulness of four postures—sitting, standing, walking, and lying down—deepens our awareness. Most of the time we talk about sitting and walking meditation, but we do not talk very much about standing and lying down. Since all postures are equally important, the Buddha never fails to mention all four in his instructions on mindfulness practice.

Venerable Ananda is not the only disciple of the Buddha to have achieved enlightenment through mindfulness of physical movements.

Venerable Cakkhupala, another of the Buddha's followers, reached enlightenment while walking mindfully. I give complete instructions for walking as a mindfulness meditation later in this chapter. First, let's talk about mindfulness of sitting.

Sitting

When we sit to meditate, we adopt a posture and then make a contour survey of the body, checking to see that the upper body, the part above the waist, is upright and straight. The body should be held in a relaxed way, without being rigid. The hands are cupped with palms up and placed on the lap, right palm on the left and the thumbs touching. The eyes are closed or left half-open, especially if falling asleep is a problem.

So which posture is best for sitting meditation?

Full lotus. In the introduction to the Four Foundations of Mindfulness Sutta, no posture is mentioned other than full lotus. In this position, both knees touch the floor. The legs are crossed at the calf. The left foot rests on the right thigh, and the right foot rests on the left thigh. The soles of both feet are turned upward like the petals of a lotus.

When we sit correctly in this position, the body is very stable. The spine is straight, and the lungs expand and contract smoothly. Blood circulation is good, at least in the upper part of the body. Normally when the mind and body are relaxed, it is easy to fall asleep. But when we are sitting in full lotus, we fall asleep less often because the body remains securely upright.

For many people, full lotus is not an easy position. But any skill we try to learn can be difficult at the beginning. For instance, we probably fell many times when we were learning to ride a bicycle. By repeating the same activity day after day, gradually we gain proficiency. To get used to sitting in full lotus, try holding the position for one minute a day for several days. Don't expect to sit without pain. After a few days, increase the time to a couple of minutes, and continue to lengthen the time gradually day by day. Keep in mind that the posture won't be perfect immediately.

For many years, I sat in the half lotus posture I describe below. When I was sixty-five, one day I thought, "Let me try full lotus." I held the posture for only five minutes. It was really painful! I thought the blood circulation would be cut off in my legs, and I would get gangrene resulting in amputation! As soon as this thought arose in my mind, I changed my posture and sat in half lotus as usual. But the next day I tried again. This time I was able to sit for about eight minutes before the pain started. After ten minutes, the pain became unbearable. However, rather than changing my position immediately, I determined to sit a little longer. Although I had been sitting in half lotus for forty-five years, within three weeks I could sit in full lotus for half an hour.

Many healthy people can learn to sit in full lotus if they persist in their efforts as I did. However, people with physical problems should not force themselves to sit in this posture.

Half lotus. In this posture, both knees touch the floor. One leg lies flat on the floor from knee to foot. The foot of the other leg rests on top of the opposite thigh, with the sole turned upward. Many people can develop proficiency with the half lotus by the same gradual process I have described.

Burmese posture. In this posture, both legs lie flat on the floor from knee to foot. The lower legs are parallel, with one leg placed in front of the other and feet uncrossed. This posture is reasonably comfortable. Most people can learn to sit in this position without too much difficulty.

Easy style. The right foot is tucked under the left knee, and the left foot is tucked under the right knee. Many people can sit in this position for some time.

Using a meditation bench. If none of these postures are comfortable, it is also possible to kneel on a meditation bench. The feet are tucked under the bench, and the knees are on the floor. The bench goes across your shins, enabling you to sit comfortably in a kneeling posture without putting pressure on your feet.

Sitting in a chair. Some people find it impossible to sit comfortably in any of these postures. They may sit on a chair, placing the feet flat on the floor close to each other. In this posture, the back should be straight and not leaning against the back support of the chair.

MINDFULNESS OF SITTING

As we sit, we become aware of the feeling of the posture we have chosen and that the feeling changes over time. Changes actually begin the moment the body makes contact with the cushion, bench, or chair. When the body touches anything, we feel the touching. In that touch we notice the hardness or softness of the seat. Hardness and softness are characteristics of the earth element. The feeling that arises from contact with the seat is generally pleasant at first. But as it continues, the feeling often changes from pleasant, to neutral, to unpleasant or even painful.

We observe this. Then we notice that nobody is controlling these changes. They happen by themselves. The mind wants to remain calm and peaceful, experiencing the progress of our meditation. In spite of this wish, the feeling of the posture changes. Paying attention to these changes reminds us that the four elements are impermanent, as are our feelings and perceptions.

After we sit for a while, we feel the heat of our buttocks or thighs. As the heat radiates, the seat becomes warm. Soon the heat from our body and the heat from the seat make the whole body feel warm. Experiencing this, we are mindful of the heat element. On hot days, we may perspire. Sweat arises from the body's water element. So we are mindful of this element. We also experience movements associated with the breathing cycle, such as the rising and falling of the abdomen and chest. Sometimes we feel intestinal gas. These movements make us mindful of the air element.

To maintain whatever sitting posture we have adopted, we use mental energy that arises naturally from our knowledge that things are always changing. If this energy stops, we slouch, fall asleep, or lose our balance. As we watch these changes, we try not to become upset or disappointed. For instance, we avoid the thoughts "How can I meditate when I am in pain?" and "I'll never be able to sit in full lotus!"

We are also mindful of the five aggregates. The body is the form aggregate. The sensations that arise due to contact with the seat belong to the feeling aggregate. Our minds register changes that are occurring due to the perception aggregate. The thoughts that arise regarding our sitting, body, contact, feelings, and perceptions come from the thought aggregate, as does our attention to what is taking place. We become aware of all of these occurrences because of the consciousness aggregate.

We also become aware of the five aggregates cooperating with one another. When our posture changes, our feelings, perceptions, thoughts, and consciousness also change. No permanently existing entity causes these changes to happen. The aggregates change depending on each other, not independently or because *I* have caused the changes to happen.

The mind does not need to keep observing one object to see the completion of the three steps of change—rising moment, peak moment, and passing away moment. Mindfulness and concentration, working together, can notice countless changes taking place simultaneously. Deep mindfulness sheds light on the unmistaken nature of these changes. Sitting postures are best for gaining this insight.

STANDING

We can continue our meditation in a standing posture. Mindfully and slowly, we get up from sitting. We notice that mental activity generates sufficient physical energy to lift the body from its sitting position.

Standing, we relax our body and hands. The body is straight, the feet are parallel, and the spinal column is upright, just as it was when we were sitting. We breathe mindfully. We pay attention to the feeling of the posture and to the contact between the feet and the floor. We do not allow the body to sway. We have relaxed awareness of our breath, feelings, and consciousness.

We notice how the feeling of the standing position changes from comfortable to neutral and then to uncomfortable. We notice our changing perception of these feelings. When thoughts arise regarding the body, feelings, and perceptions, we notice them with attention, which is also a thought. We notice how the thoughts change. We are mindful of our conscious awareness of these changes. Thus, while standing, we are aware of the five aggregates and their changes.

We are aware that whatever we are experiencing is impermanent, unsatisfactory, and selfless. Our awareness of these factors reminds us that, "This is not *mine*, this is not *I*, this is not *myself*." Here "this" means whatever we are experiencing at the moment. We realize that it is neither some special being inside us nor some external being that does the standing. Rather, standing takes place dependent on various causes and conditions. One of these is our intention to stand up and remain standing. Intention is also caused by something else. Previously the sitting posture became uncomfortable. In order to relieve this discomfort, a desire arose for us to stand up.

Energy is necessary to keep the body in a standing position. When our energy is low, we cannot remain standing, as we have all experienced. The mind generates energy through intention. That energy is an aspect of the air element created by our mental activities. We also become aware of the air element through our breath going in and out.

We are mindful of the other elements as well. The bones and muscles holding us upright belong to the earth element. We also experience the earth element in the touch of our feet on the floor. When we stand in a particular place for a few minutes, friction between the feet and the floor causes that spot to become warm, and we feel the heat element under our feet. We feel the water element there, too, in the form of perspiration. Thus all four elements are working together smoothly and dependently.

At the same time, we have to remain alert and not fall asleep. Although we can stand habitually, if we are mindful, we become aware of everything that is involved in standing. This awareness is what the Buddha means when he says, "When standing, understand standing." Although even children and animals know how to stand, they do not understand fully what is taking place.

We stand for maybe one minute, two minutes, three minutes, or as long as we feel comfortable in this position. We stand up while breathing. While we are standing, we are breathing. We never stop noticing the breath.

WALKING

From the standing posture, if we choose, we can begin walking meditation. Mindfulness helps us notice that walking is really a sequence of nine actions:

1. We begin by standing for a couple of minutes, relaxing the hands and body and focusing on our breathing.

2. We lift the heel of one foot—let's say, the left foot.

3. We rest the left foot on its toes. We are mindful of the contact of the toes with the floor and the feeling arising from that contact. We notice how the feeling changes as the contact changes.

4. We lift the left foot.

5. We move the left foot forward. We notice that the feeling we had while standing is no longer there when we lift the heel of the left foot. Likewise, the feeling that we had while lifting the heel is no longer there when we rest the left foot on its toes. Now, new feelings arise as we lift the whole foot and move it forward. The thoughts "this is the foot; this is the movement; this is the forward motion; this is the change" arise, remain briefly, and pass away. Until the left foot is placed on the floor and firmly settled, we balance the body on the right foot. If we become unmindful, we lose the balance.

6. The forward motion of the left foot stops.

7. We lower the left foot.

8. We touch the left foot to the ground.

9. Finally, we press the left foot against the ground.

10. Then the cycle of movements, feelings, perceptions, and thoughts begins again with the other foot.

In order to notice these tiny changes, we need to walk slowly. When our movements are deliberate and unhurried, we can observe each aspect of walking in detail. Walking slowly is like a slow-motion replay at a football game. Though the spectators might not see a penalty take place on the field because the players are moving too quickly, watching the replay slows down the action and allows the referee to make the correct call.

In the same way, when we walk at our usual rapid pace, it's hard to observe what's really happening. Slow and mindful walking gives the mind the opportunity to become aware of each small change in the body's position and in the other aggregates that alter as a result. It's relatively easier to notice these differences while we are sitting, because the body is not moving.

Only through mindful attention can we notice that every time we move a foot forward, new contact, feeling, thought, perception, and attention arise, and old contact, feeling, thought, perception, and attention pass away. We may not be aware of all these things when we first start to practice walking meditation, but with gradual training, we are able to see at least some of the things that are taking place.

MINDFULNESS OF WALKING

We walk slowly not only so that we can observe the details of the movements but also so that we can watch what is going on in our minds. The purpose of walking meditation is not training the body but rather, through using the physical activity of walking, to train the mind.

For this reason, though we are mindful of each movement as we walk, we do not verbalize silently what we are observing. Words come between our mental awareness and what is happening. Moreover, too many things are happening simultaneously to name them. And some of these things are so subtle that we will not find words for them, or we may be noticing things for the first time.

For instance, though we observe the movements of our feet, we don't have to say, "left, right, left, right," as if we were marching in the army. Nor should we say "lifting, lifting, lifting" when we lift each foot. We simply become aware of these movements directly, without words. The same is true of changes taking place in our feelings, perceptions, thoughts, and consciousness. We notice these without saying, "changing, changing, changing." When unintentional bodily activities flow smoothly, the mind is trained to be patient and develops deeper mindfulness.

However, we may need to verbalize some thoughts and emotions, especially those that distract us from focusing on what is happening. If a thought or emotion such as greed, anger, delusion, jealousy, fear, or worry arises, we use mindfulness to remove it as quickly as possible. For instance, if anger arises, we pay attention to it. But if the anger does not pass away by itself, we think in words to try to discover the cause of the anger. It is like having a silent conversation. Because we are mindful, we are careful not to blame anybody—neither ourselves nor someone else.

While we are walking, we are also mindful of our breathing. Coordinating the breath with the movement of the feet is possible only when we do not verbalize each event. With attention, we notice that the breath is flowing in and out and the feet are moving at the same time. Below I give detailed instructions for practicing walking meditation coordinated with the breath.

What We Learn

It's amazing how many activities of the body and mind we can train ourselves to notice while doing something we usually take for granted, like walking. These activities never stop. They have been going on and changing continually since the moment we were conceived. Observing the tiny changes that take place during each step helps us become aware that the body, the mind, and everything else is inescapably impermanent.

We also see that walking is an interdependently arising action that is made up of many other interdependent actions and events. At the speed of lightning, the intention to walk arises. Along with the intention, the heel lifts. The movement of the foot takes place so quickly that if we don't pay close attention, we nearly miss it. So we become aware that intention and attention seem to happen simultaneously.

Similarly, it is hard to notice intention apart from physical movements, such as lifting the heel. It all takes place so quickly, like the light that turns on when we flip the switch. However, with attention, we can learn to see the difference between the intention and the action that results. Very slowly, very mindfully, we notice the intention to breathe in, the intention to breathe out, the intention to lift one foot, the intention to move it forward, and so on. Since the mind is fully occupied by observing all this, it does not wander.

When we are mindful of walking as it actually is, it is also easier to understand that it is not a self or soul that does the walking. All of this activity has not been made possible by some permanent being inside us. It arises interdependently because of causes and conditions, which we can train ourselves to notice.

KEY POINTS FOR WALKING MEDITATION

Though you can practice walking meditation anywhere, a private place is best. Make sure there is enough space for you to walk at least five to ten paces in a straight line, though this is the bare minimum distance. Ideally, the walking distance should be much longer; some meditation centers have thirty-foot long walking paths.

- Begin in the standing posture. Focus on your breathing.

- Inhale and lift the heel of one foot.

- Exhale and rest that foot on its toes.

- Inhale as you lift that foot and move it forward.

- Exhale as you bring that foot down and touch the floor.

- Repeat this sequence with the other foot.

- After five to ten paces, rest in standing posture for one minute, turn around, stand again for another minute, and repeat the sequence to walk back to where you started.

- As you walk, keep your head up and your neck relaxed. Walk slowly and naturally. Keep your eyes open to maintain balance, but avoid looking at anything in particular.

- Strive to be mindful of as many of the changes taking place in your body and mind as you can.

▸ Once you have grasped the technique of slow walking, you can speed up slightly. But don't walk too quickly. A good pace is one inhalation and one exhalation per step. Inhale while lifting the heel of one foot, resting it on its toes, lifting the whole foot, and moving it forward. Then, stop. While exhaling, lower the foot, touch the floor, and press it against the floor. Again, stop. Repeat the sequence with the other foot. After a while, the breath and the movement of the feet become almost automatic.

LYING DOWN

When the mind and body are relaxed, as they are during sitting meditation, it's easy to fall asleep. Imagine how easy it is to fall asleep while meditating in a lying down posture!

Nevertheless, I recommend this posture in a few circumstances. Most obviously, people who are so sick that they cannot sit up without pain can lie on their backs, with arms and legs extended, and meditate using the breath as the primary focus. The lying down posture can also be helpful for people who can't sleep because of a sinus condition or other painful problem. They may find relief by lying on their backs and meditating on how the uncomfortable sensations they are experiencing arise, remain, and pass away. While focusing on the impermanence of the sensations, they should take care to avoid feelings of resentment or depression.

I have suffered from difficulty sleeping because of sinus problems for many years. I lie on my back and meditate on the impermanence of the feelings. In ten or fifteen minutes, I fall asleep. Finally, even people with no physical problems can benefit from practicing mindfulness meditation on the breath while lying down in bed before going to sleep.

As is important in all postures, while lying down, we understand that we are lying down. We remember that there has been an intention to lie down and that the mind has generated the energy to do so. We are aware of the earth element in the contact between the body and the bed, the heat element that arises, as well as the water and air elements.

While lying down, as in every posture we have discussed, we use attention to build awareness that the five aggregates are impermanent, unsatisfactory, and selfless. We use mindfulness of everything that is taking place as a buffer against anger, resentment, lust, jealousy, fear, tension, and every other unwholesome thought and emotion. Of course, it is not easy to maintain clear awareness of lying down for very long, because this is the posture that we use most of the time to go to sleep. But until we fall asleep, we can remain mindful.

And like Ananda and many other followers of the Buddha, we can strive in every posture to have mindfulness that is so pure, sharp, and powerful that we progress toward liberation.

3: *Clear Comprehension*

When the Buddha was explaining the meaning of domain, one of the aspects of clear comprehension, he told the following story:

"In the Himalayas, the king of mountains, there are rugged and uneven zones where neither monkeys nor human beings can go, rugged and uneven zones where monkeys can go but not human beings, and flat and delightful regions where both monkeys and human beings can go. There, along the monkey trails, hunters set out traps of sticky pitch.

"A monkey who is not foolish sees the pitch and avoids it from afar. But a foolish monkey seizes the pitch with his hand and gets stuck there. Thinking, 'I will free my hand,' the monkey seizes the pitch with his other hand. Thinking, 'I will free both hands,' he seizes the pitch with his foot. Thinking, 'I will free both hands and my foot,' he seizes it with his other foot. Thinking, 'I will free both hands and feet,' he applies his muzzle to the pitch as well.

"Thus, bhikkhus, that monkey lies there screeching, trapped at five points. He has met with calamity and disaster, and the hunter can do with him as he wishes. So it is, bhikkhus, when one strays outside one's own domain into the domain of others. . . .

"What is the domain of others? It is the five cords of sensual pleasure. . .

"And what is a bhikkhu's own domain? It is the Four Foundations of Mindfulness."

(tr. Bhikkhu Bodhi)

THIS STORY illustrates an essential element of the Buddha's message: every calamity or disaster we experience begins with our own unwise actions. If we want to end our suffering, we must look carefully at the activities of our own body and mind. This is the laboratory where we must work very hard.

With the instruments of mindfulness and clear comprehension, we investigate our body, feelings, perceptions, thoughts, and consciousness— not as a biologist, chemist, or pathologist, but more profoundly, as a meditator, whose aims are morality, spiritual development, and deep insight. In every activity, whether we are sitting, standing, walking, lying down, talking, eating, or meditating, mindfulness and clear comprehension work together to help us see that whatever we are experiencing is temporary and thus can never bring us lasting satisfaction. Moreover, though we may think we understand perfectly what is happening, often we are confused and deluded.

So what is clear comprehension?

Traditionally, it has four aspects: purpose, suitability, domain, and non-delusion. In brief, *purpose* means that there is a good reason for us to engage in the activity. *Suitability* means that the activity fulfills that purpose. *Domain*, as we see from the story of the foolish monkey, means that the activity lies within appropriate boundaries. Finally, *non-delusion* means that while we are doing the activity, we are investigating whether we understand clearly what is really going on.

Purpose. When we do something, we generally have a purpose in mind. We go to a particular shop to buy an item that we need. We arrange to meet someone to conduct business or have a conversation or share a meal.

But when we engage in mindfulness meditation, our purpose is not an ordinary one, like going to the grocery store or the office. Instead, our goal is very specific and very special. According to the Buddha, we practice meditation

- to purify the mind,
- to overcome sorrow and lamentation,
- to end grief and despair,
- to progress on the path toward liberation, and
- to attain liberation and the end of suffering.

Let's look at each to understand the Buddha's meaning.

Purify the mind. The first purpose of meditation is purification. Very strong mindfulness can be compared to detergent. Just as we must wash a dirty plate before we can use it to eat healthy food, we must clear away impure mental states, such as hatred, greed, and delusion, before we can develop pure states, such as generosity, loving-friendliness, and wisdom.

The Buddha compared the process to what happens when we dye cloth: "O bhikkhus, just as an impure, stained cloth, when dyed blue, yellow, or red, takes a bad hue and an impure color because the cloth is impure and stained, in the same manner, when the mind is defiled, a bad state can be expected. Just as a pure, unstained cloth, when dyed blue, yellow, or red, takes a pure color and a bright hue, so when the mind is pure, a good state can be expected." As the sutta tells us, when the householder Upali's mind had been purified so that it was ready, receptive, elated, and confident, the Buddha taught him the Four Noble Truths:

> Just as a clean cloth with all marks removed would take dye evenly, so too, while the householder Upali sat there, the spotless immaculate vision of the Dhamma arose in him.
>
> (tr. Bhikkhu Bodhi)

The impure states that stain the mind include anger, lust, jealousy, skeptical doubt in the Dhamma, selfishness, stubbornness, and negligence. Mindfulness and clear comprehension help us eliminate these and similar unhealthy mental habits and replace them with knowledge of the Buddha's path and clarity about what we must do, and not do, to advance along it.

Overcome sorrow and lamentation. We don't meditate to weep or lament. When sad emotions arise, we might use mindfulness to look for the reason. We often find that our unhappiness is rooted in attachment to some person, position, place, or thing. Then we ask, "Why am I attached?" When we investigate carefully, we discover, "I am attached because I have forgotten that everything is impermanent. Foolishly, I think that the object of my attachment will bring me lasting happiness, pleasure, or security."

Other times we cry because we are remembering sad or traumatic events or someone else's suffering. In this case, we try to emulate the example of the Buddha. Though he saw very clearly the suffering of billions of living beings, he never wept, because he knew his sorrow could do nothing to relieve the suffering. Rather, he maintained unshakable mindfulness and perfect equanimity.

From a state of emotional balance, we can more easily see that the sad experiences of the past are no longer present. Moreover, anything we are attached to today will definitely change or pass away, without our control and without advance warning. The same is true of the joys and sufferings of others. Knowing this, our sorrow and lamentation slowly fade. Training ourselves to face this reality is the second purpose of mindfulness meditation.

End grief and despair. Grief and despair are more durable than sorrow and lamentation, so they take more effort to overcome. Sometimes, though we try to calm the mind through meditation, we cannot escape these emotions. We want to forget them; we honestly wish not to dwell on them, but they keep surfacing.

To end them, we use the same mental training I have described. We contemplate the impermanent nature of everything in life. Every past experience is already behind us. Nothing we have right now can bring us satisfaction forever. Everyone we hold dear, every attractive situation, and every pleasing moment will vanish someday. Nothing we do can prevent these changes from happening. These thoughts help us to see that our despair is a "dependent arising." It depends for its existence on causes and conditions that arise, remain for a time, and then disappear. When we use mindfulness to train the mind to accept this reality, these emotions, too, slowly fade away.

Progress on the path toward liberation. The fourth reason for practicing mindfulness is to follow the Buddha's Noble Eightfold Path, the only sure road to freedom from sorrow, lamentation, grief, and despair. I say more about the Eightfold Path in the section on mindfulness of dhamma, but in brief, the eight steps are a comprehensive guide to a life based on right understanding, thinking, speech, action, livelihood, effort, mindfulness, and concentration.

In the context of the special purposes of meditation, it is important that we recognize that we cannot separate mindfulness practice from the Buddha's path to liberation. Though some people might say, "Vipassana and insight meditation have nothing to do with Buddhism," this is not correct. As our practice deepens and the mind becomes pure and clean, we cannot fail to see the connection between meditation and every step of the Buddha's Noble Eightfold Path.

Attain liberation and the end of suffering. The final purpose of meditation is to free ourselves from the never-ending suffering of this life and future lives. Liberation is the supreme goal of mindfulness meditation; everything else is peripheral and ephemeral. A serious practitioner keeps this purpose in mind at all times—whether sitting, walking, standing, eating, drinking, talking, observing silence, taking a shower, or using the toilet!

Keeping the lofty goal of our practice of clear comprehension in mind keeps us from getting sidetracked by trivial concerns. Discussing whether some superficial aspect of our practice is or is not suitable wastes our time and distracts us from our real purpose. Since our goal is nothing short of liberation and the end of suffering, we must avoid the sticky traps of confusion and focus on the supreme goal of our practice. When we do, our mindfulness practice bears fruit very quickly.

SUITABILITY

The second aspect of clear comprehension is making sure that our activities are morally wholesome and suitable for achieving our spiritual goals. We choose a job that gives us enough time to meditate and avoid associating with people who cause harm to themselves or others. We practice right speech and refrain from conversations that interfere with our ability to concentrate. We make healthy lifestyle choices, such as eating moderately and not sleeping too much.

We also make sure that our meditation practice is well suited to our temperament. If we habitually feel agitated or overly energetic, we choose a peaceful practice that calms the mind, such as sitting down to meditate and counting the breath. Conversely, if we tend to feel drowsy and lethargic, we engage in a practice that rouses our energy, such as walking meditation. We also assess continually how well our practice is working. For instance, we ask ourselves, "Am I really concentrating and gaining insights or just sleeping on the cushion?"

Similarly, we select subjects for contemplation that help us overcome unhealthy mental habits. For instance, a person who is troubled by jealousy might experiment to see whether thinking about generosity—open-handed giving with no expectation of return—or about appreciative joy—rejoicing in the good fortune of others—is the most effective way to counteract the jealousy. Since our time is limited and our spiritual aim is lofty, we must use good judgment and be selective. As the Buddha said, "Do not strive everywhere."

DOMAIN

The third aspect of clear comprehension is practicing right thinking so that we remain within appropriate boundaries—our own domain or field. Allowing the mind to wander into "delightful regions" is dangerous, as illustrated by the story of the monkey trap told at the beginning of this chapter. If the foolish monkey had stayed within his proper domain, he would not have been tempted by the sticky pitch and would not have become trapped at five points and bound by five cords of sensual pleasure.

What are those points and those cords? They are the five kinds of sense consciousness and their five desirable objects: lovely forms cognizable by the eye, agreeable sounds cognizable by the ear, enticing smells cognizable by the nose, tantalizing tastes cognizable by the tongue, and pleasing touches cognizable by the body.

If the mind goes astray as we engage in meditation, we bring our focus back to the five aggregates as we are experiencing them right now—our body and posture, feelings, perceptions, thoughts, and consciousness. These are the appropriate fields of the Four Foundations of Mindfulness. For example, if the thought of an attractive object arises, we reflect on it mindfully without getting involved in the details. We avoid emotional reactions, and mental or verbal commentaries, such as whether it is male or female, beautiful or ugly, enticing or disturbing. We think only that this is an impermanent object. We do the same with every other sight, sound, smell, taste, touch, and thought.

As the Buddha admonished his followers: "Monks, be islands unto yourselves; be a refuge unto yourselves with no other refuge. Let the Dhamma be your island . . . having put aside hankering and fretting for the world."

Non-delusion

The fourth clear comprehension is non-delusion. This aspect is more difficult to understand. As we have noted, we are deluded when we think that the objects of our attachment will bring us permanent happiness and satisfaction. We are also deluded when we think that the people and situations that provoked our angry feelings will always infuriate us. However, it's harder to see that these delusions arise because of a deeper and more troublesome source of confusion—the notion of a permanently existing self.

At a conventional level, it is certainly true that *I* engage in many activities, such as walking forward and backward, eating, drinking, sleeping, wearing clothes, talking, and remaining silent. *I* also experience emotions, perceive sensations, and engage in many other activities with *my* body and mind. But as mindfulness meditation reveals, no activity takes places independently. Rather, everything and everyone that exists depends on a wide variety of simultaneous causes and conditions that come into existence, remain present, and then pass away.

Since everything arises interdependently, no separate self or soul causes an activity like walking to happen, as we see very clearly when we practice walking meditation. In the same way, there is no part of the body or mind that is inherently *me* and no possession or person that is permanently *mine*. Our feelings of attachment and anger start to fade when we recognize that there is no independently existing *I* to feel attached to *him* or angry with *her*.

We use terms like *I, we, self, soul, you, me, he, she, him, her* to make understanding easier. These are conventional terms coined by human beings to facilitate communication, but just because they are useful doesn't mean they refer to any independent and unchanging thing findable in the world.

Insight into this unmistaken truth about reality is known in Buddhism as "emptiness of self" or *sunnata*. Clear comprehension of this truth arises from our accumulated meditative experience of observing what is really happening from moment to moment in our body and mind. When we come to see that everything, including ourselves, is impermanent, unsatisfactory, and selfless, we have achieved clear comprehension of non-delusion.

Lost and Found Mindfulness

Another aspect of clear comprehension of non-delusion is very immediate and practical. Sometimes when we practice mindfulness, we delude ourselves with naive and foolish thinking. For instance, say we are practicing walking meditation. Suddenly we notice that twenty minutes have passed and we have walked two or three miles without mindfulness and clear comprehension. It may occur to us that we should go back to the point where we lost our mindfulness and pick it up!

That thought is deluded. Is mindfulness a tangible thing that we can drop at a certain time and place and then go back and pick up? Mindfulness is a mental state. Once a mental state is lost, we will never find it again. Lost mindfulness is gone forever. We were simply distracted. Probably we don't remember what distracted us or where or when this happened. Instead of returning to an imaginary point in time and space, the moment we remember that our mindfulness has been lost, we should begin again to be mindful.

The same is true any time we lose our mindfulness. Suppose a monk who is practicing mindfulness eats some food and then remembers that he has not been eating mindfully. He cannot take back the food that he has already consumed and start all over with mindfulness. The sensible solution for him is to continue eating, starting right now, with more diligence and mindfulness. (By the way, I explain more about mindful eating later in this chapter.)

We can also lose and find our mindfulness in a more subtle way. Sometimes, when we are practicing mindfulness, we suddenly experience a calm and peaceful feeling. Then it may occur to us that this calm and peaceful feeling is the self. As soon as this thought arises, we should be mindful of it. When we are mindful, we notice that the calm and peaceful feeling is also changing and fading away, expressing its impermanent nature. As it passes away, the notion of self also passes away. This is how we tackle the delusion of the existence of self and practice clear comprehension of non-delusion.

Always remember: becoming mindful of losing our mindfulness *is* mindfulness. Admitting that we have been unmindful is an honest and sincere way of practicing mindfulness. If regret or embarrassment arises, we notice these mental states without self-blame or self-hatred. Even mindfulness is impermanent. Becoming aware of the impermanence of mindfulness is mindfulness itself. Understanding this truth is clear comprehension of non-delusion.

Clear Comprehension in Daily Life

We develop clear comprehension by remaining mindful not only when we meditate but also in daily life during every kind of physical, verbal, and mental activity. The Buddha did not need to make any special effort to be mindful. His comprehension was also naturally clear. He performed every action with mindfulness and clear comprehension— walking, talking, bending, sitting down, wearing robes, eating, and drinking.

As a sutta tells us, the Buddha's mindfulness is like an elephant's neck. It is always connected to the elephant's head, a symbol of wisdom. Just as the elephant protects his vulnerable neck from the attack of a lion by using his huge body, the Buddha maintained his mindfulness by using clear comprehension, morality, concentration, wisdom, liberation, and knowledge of liberation—the qualities of his body of enlightenment. The Buddha advised us to follow his example and engage in all our activities with mindfulness and clear comprehension.

We have to eat, drink, wear clothes, and exercise to stay healthy. We need sleep and shelter. But we use clear comprehension to guard against attachment to these necessities and to avoid greed, hatred, delusion, competition, jealousy, and pride.

For instance, some people wear clothes to show off their wealth or beauty, which encourages pride and attachment to the notion of self. By contrast, when they get dressed, monks and nuns train themselves to think, "I wear these clothes to protect this body from cold, heat, mosquitoes, wind, and sun, and to cover my nakedness." Similarly, when they lie down to sleep, they think, "I use this shelter and this bed to keep this body from cold, heat, mosquitoes, wind, and sun, to get rid of weariness, and to make the body comfortable." We can do the same. In these very small ways, we purify the mind and begin to free it from greed and other unwholesome states.

Clear comprehension and mindfulness also help us make positive choices concerning all other imaginable activities. For instance, someone once asked me, "Can I use my gun with clear comprehension to shoot a deer?"

I answered, "No."

"Why not?" he asked.

So I explained further. "The Buddha divided thoughts into two categories—wholesome and unwholesome. When he saw that unwholesome thoughts were not suitable for achieving his goal of liberation, he abandoned them. When he saw that wholesome thoughts were suitable for achieving this goal, he cultivated them.

"The moment even the thought of a gun occurs, a person practicing mindfulness realizes that any weapon is an instrument of cruelty. The gun reminds him of violence, hatred, greed, and delusion. Violence begets violence. Hatred begets hatred. Greed begets greed. Delusion begets delusion.

"Then he thinks, 'I have suffered from these harmful thoughts long enough. Now I am trying to get rid of my greed, hatred, and delusion through the practice of mindfulness. I should not let my mind think of using any weapon.'"

We apply the same kind of reasoning to every other activity of body, speech, and mind. Doing so is the proper way to practice clear comprehension.

CLEAR COMPREHENSION OF EATING

Now, eating and drinking, chewing, munching, swallowing, tasting— how do we practice clear comprehension of these?

First, to remind ourselves of the appropriate purpose of eating, we recite at mealtime: "With mindful reflection, I eat this food, neither for amusement, nor for intoxication, nor for the sake of physical beauty and attractiveness, but only for the endurance and continuance of this body, for ending discomfort, and for assisting the holy life, considering, 'Thus I shall terminate old feelings without arousing new feelings. I shall be healthy and blameless and shall live in comfort.'"

Then, while we are eating, we observe a few simple disciplines that reinforce our mindfulness. We eat very slowly, moving our hands to the plate slowly and taking the food slowly. We also are mindful of what is happening in the mind. If greed arises because the food is so tasty, we clearly comprehend the greed and say to ourselves: "Ah! I must be mindful! All right, this food is delicious. But all of my actions must be suitable for my spiritual goals. I will not be greedy and overeat." Needless to say, we avoid junk food for the same mindful reasons.

In the same way, when we drink hot or cold liquids, we think, "I take this drink with mindful reflection to overcome pain caused by thirst, avoid sickness, and maintain the health of this body."

Monks and nuns train themselves to observe thirty rules concerning eating and drinking to maintain clear comprehension. Below are a few guidelines inspired by these rules that anyone can use to practice mindfulness of eating and drinking.

Key Points for Mindful Eating

- I train myself to prefer healthy and nourishing food and drink.
- I train myself to eat moderately and to avoid junk food.
- I train myself to watch my mind while I am eating to avoid greed, hatred, and delusion.
- I train myself not to overfill my bowl or plate.
- I train myself to take whatever food is offered or available without being picky.
- I train myself not to look at others' food critically or with jealousy.
- I train myself to move my hands slowly.
- I train myself not to open my mouth before the food is carried to it.
- I train myself not to stuff my mouth with food.
- I train myself not to talk when I have food in my mouth.
- I train myself not to scatter food or be wasteful.
- I train myself not to smack my lips or make slurping sounds.
- I train myself not to lick my fingers.

4: *Parts and Elements*

A young monk was a student of Venerable Sariputta, one of the Buddha's senior bhikkhus. Since the young man was troubled by lust, Sariputta instructed him to go to the forest to meditate on the impurities of the body. Despite his devoted efforts, the monk found that his lust was increasing. So Sariputta took him to see the Buddha.

The Buddha handed the young monk a lily and told him to focus his mind on the flower's bright color. Using this method, the monk attained advanced states of concentration.

Because he was very pleased with the Buddha and the meditation he had suggested, the young monk developed tremendous attachment to the Buddha. As he was concentrating, he remembered the Buddha's handsome, radiant, serene, and majestic body, his sweet voice, and his wise-looking face.

Suddenly, the Buddha's image appeared in his mind, and he heard the Buddha's voice saying:

> Destroy attachment to self,
>
> As you could an autumn lily in your fist.
>
> Cultivate the path to peace,
>
> The Nirvana [Nibbana] taught by the Well-Gone-One.

When he opened his eyes, the young monk saw that the beautiful lily, once so bright, fresh, and lively, had withered away.

So he meditated on the impermanence of the beauty, freshness, and life of the lily. Reflecting that his own handsome, young, healthy, and strong body would grow old and wither just as the flower had, he attained liberation from attachment to his body, feelings, perceptions, thoughts, and consciousness.

WHEN WE LOOK at ourselves in the mirror, we normally feel proud of the parts of our body that appear handsome or beautiful and displeased by those that seem old or unattractive. Judgments like these lead to attachment to the parts that we like, such as our shiny hair, and hatred of those we dislike, such as our crooked teeth.

This chapter focuses on learning to look at the body differently. Through mindfulness, we train ourselves to see the body impartially, as a collection of thirty-two parts—not just the external parts we can see in the mirror, but also the internal parts, such as the bones, liver, and blood. As we discover, each of these parts is either solid like the earth element or liquid like the water element. Like all other material objects, each of these parts is always changing. In fact, they are all as impermanent as the "autumn lily" in the young monk's vision of the Buddha.

In practical terms, meditation on the body's parts and elements opens the mind to accepting our body as it is right now, without our usual emotional reactions. It helps us overcome pride and self-hatred and regard our body with the balanced mind of equanimity. The Buddha gave an example to illustrate this point:

> Suppose there is a bag full of different types of grain—rice, hill rice, paddy rice, lentils, green peas, barley, sesame seed, and mustard seed. When a man with good eyesight looks into the bag, he identifies the various grains, saying, "This is rice, hill rice, paddy rice, lentils, green peas, barley, sesame seed, and mustard seed." He does not say, "This is barley. I hate barley." Nor does he say, "This is sesame seed. I love sesame seed."

We train in mindfulness so that we can see ourselves clearly, like the man with good eyesight. We discover that because every part of the body is subject to illness, injury, and death, no part can give us lasting satisfaction. Most important, we find that there is no being or person in any of the parts of the body or mind that we can identify as *me*. From this we learn that the body is selfless. With the Buddha's example in mind, we might call this method of meditation "going against the grain," as it runs counter to our ordinary way of viewing the body.

We should approach this subject of meditation cautiously, since meditating on our body or the bodies of others without proper mindfulness can lead to attachment, as happened to the student of Sariputta. Other emotions such as dislike, even hatred, can also occur if we are unmindful. Our intention should be to see the parts of the body as they are without distortion and to know that they are neither beautiful nor ugly but simply pieces of an ever-changing process.

THE FIRST FIVE PARTS

Traditionally, the body is divided into thirty-two parts. The whole list is given a little later in this chapter. To begin, we focus our mindfulness on just five parts: the head hairs, body hairs, nails, teeth, and skin. We start with these parts because they are so conspicuous; when we meet a person, these catch our eye first. We also spend a lot of money to decorate and improve these parts. We change our hair color, whiten our teeth, and get facial treatments to feel more attractive, but also, perhaps, to deceive others about our real appearance.

We can easily use these five parts to stand for the whole body, since every other part can be found between the hair on the head and the nails on the toes. Mindful contemplation of even one of these parts can be enough for some people to gain insight. So, for example, when we reflect with clear comprehension on our head hair, we see that it is always changing. We then apply this insight to all other parts of the body, recognizing that what happens to the visible parts happens to the invisible ones as well.

Here are some ways to begin meditating mindfully about the first five parts:

Head hair. Since hair is so visible and so present to our minds, it's easy to see the changes that take place in our hair day-by-day and year-by-year. On Monday, our hair may be soft and pretty looking, but by Tuesday, if we haven't washed it, it can be stringy or even smelly! Over the years, hair changes even more. Our dark brown hair turns grey or white, or it falls out, prematurely showing our scalp.

We can deepen this insight by thinking about how easily our attitude toward hair shifts, depending on where it is. Does it make sense to be proud of hair on the head given that we throw out a whole bowl of soup if one hair falls into it? And though we find hair in our food disgusting, hair can also be used for holy purposes. According to legend, a princess known as Hemamala hid the Buddha's tooth in her hair knot so that nobody could steal it and brought it to Sri Lanka. When we reflect on the nature of hair with clear comprehension, it doesn't matter whether the hair is on the head or in the bowl of soup or hiding a holy relic: our attitude toward it is the same.

Body hair. Our attitude toward hair on the body is similarly changeable. A man can be vain about his beard, cutting it, twisting it, growing it, and shaving it to make it look attractive. But the same beard would be repulsive if it were separated from the body. Women also spend time and money changing the shape of their eyebrows and removing unwanted body hair. Considering these points, we recognize: "Hair is just hair. Wherever on the body it is, or isn't, it has no intrinsic meaning. Moreover, the hair on the body is not *mine*. It is not *I* and not my self. It is as impermanent as everything else in this body and mind. It vanishes. It is empty."

Nails. So long as nails are on our fingers and toes, they are attractive. Some people decorate them colorfully to improve their appearance. Nails are useful because they protect our toes and fingertips. But toenail clippings are certainly not very beautiful! Fingernails collect dirt when we work with our hands and dead skin when we scratch our head, the soles of our feet, or our ears. Young, strong, and healthy-looking nails become old, yellowed, and brittle as we age. Fungus, ingrown nails, and other conditions are the source of pain and suffering. Thinking about the nails in this way, we recognize that they are impermanent and unsatisfactory. They are not *I* and not my self.

Teeth. Teeth are more useful than head hair, body hair, and nails. We are very happy when our teeth are strong and healthy. But teeth can make us very unhappy. Many people are afraid of going to the dentist. We can easily recall the last time we sat in the dentist's chair to have a tooth pulled. Once the tooth comes out, no matter how useful, strong, and beautiful it was, it becomes ugly and useless. Though the dentist puts the tooth in our palm, we don't want to bring it home. Like every other part of the body, teeth are impermanent and unsatisfactory. Though it was once in *my* mouth, a tooth is not *myself*.

Skin. Skin can be a sign of beauty, but only if it is a certain color and is unwrinkled. Of course, the color that is considered beautiful changes depending on where we live! Skin is also useful. We experience hardness, softness, roughness, and smoothness because of touch information we receive through the skin. Skin also regulates body temperature. When we are hot, the skin expands, and the body cools itself through perspiration that pours through the skin. Skin-to-skin contact is so important to newborn babies that they can die if they are not touched.

But the skin is also a source of suffering. Rashes and other skin diseases make us very uncomfortable. In spite of skin care treatments and cosmetics, skin also wrinkles, sags, and darkens as we age. Every day, our skin dries up and dies. Ordinary house dust is full of dead skin! Many people experience discrimination because of their skin color.

Considering these points, we conclude: "Like every other part of the body, skin is neither beautiful nor ugly. It is useful but also a cause of suffering. It is, therefore, impermanent and unsatisfactory. It is not *mine. I* am not this. This is not my self."

MINDFULNESS OF THE THIRTY-TWO PARTS

The parts of the body we have been considering so far are the first five of thirty-two parts. These are traditionally divided into groups. The first twenty parts belong to the body's earth element. These are divided into four groups of five. The last twelve parts belong to the body's water element. They are divided into two groups of six.

What follows is the traditional division. Below that, I suggest a method for getting started with mindfulness meditation on the thirty-two parts of the body.

Twenty Parts Belonging to the Body's Earth Element
- head hairs, body hairs, nails, teeth, skin
- flesh, sinews, bones, bone marrow, kidneys
- heart, liver, diaphragm, spleen, lungs
- large intestines, small intestines, contents of the stomach, feces, brain

Twelve Parts Belonging to the Body's Water Element
- bile, phlegm, pus, blood, sweat, fat
- tears, lymph, saliva, mucus, joint fluid, urine

KEY POINTS FOR MEDITATION ON THE THIRTY-TWO PARTS OF THE BODY

Meditating on the parts of the body can help you take care of yourself calmly when things go wrong. Sometimes it is possible to accelerate healing by focusing your mind on a diseased part to send it positive body chemicals. To do so, you need strong attention, concentration, and visualization, which this meditation helps to develop. Another benefit is that when you understand the true nature of the body, you are not upset even by the thought of death.

▸ Begin meditating by cultivating loving-friendliness toward all beings.

▸ Remind yourself that your intention in meditating on the thirty-two parts of the body is to overcome pride and self-hatred for your own body and lust and loathing for the bodies of others. You want to regard all bodies and their parts with the balanced mind of equanimity.

▸ Meditate on the first five parts belonging to the earth element using thoughts similar to those I have suggested. Stay with these five until they become very clear in your mind.

▸ Then meditate on the next five parts. Contemplate these the same way. For instance, remember how important your bones are. They hold you upright when you stand and make walking and all other physical activities possible. But bones can also be the source of suffering, as anyone who has broken an arm or a leg has experienced.

▸ Next, combine the first two groups together and meditate on the first ten. Continue to add other groups until you complete the twenty parts of the body belonging to the earth element.

▸ Keep in mind that simply repeating the names of the body parts does not do any good. Use your imagination to visualize those parts that are hidden under the skin. Consider each with thoughts similar to those we used for the first five.

▸ Then add the first group of six liquid parts of the body and meditate on them until they become clear in your mind. Finally, add the remaining group of six.

▸ As you meditate on the last twelve parts, remember that none of them makes you especially proud or helps you make a good impression on others. However, like all other parts of the body, your liquid parts are essential and useful. Remembering this point helps you to overcome revulsion.

▸ If any part is not clear to you, drop it for the moment and focus on those parts that are clear. Once you have established mindfulness on the clear parts, go back to the hazy parts and meditate until they, too, become clear.

▸ How long you should meditate on each part or group varies. Some people take longer than others to achieve mindfulness and clear comprehension.

▸ Remember that your aim is to recognize that each of the thirty-two parts of the body is impermanent. Because it is subject to growth, decay, disease, and death, it cannot give you lasting satisfaction. Finally, recognize that each is "not *mine*, not *I*, and not my self."

MINDFULNESS OF THE BODY'S ELEMENTS

We have already mentioned the four elements—earth, water, heat, and air—in connection with mindfulness of breathing and mindfulness of postures. As I have explained, the thirty-two parts of the body are divided between the earth element and water element. The parts connected to these elements are tangible, which makes them easier to use to develop mindfulness. The heat element and air element are harder to visualize. However, meditating on these elements is also important to mindfulness of the body because they are responsible for essential life processes such as digestion and circulation.

The body's elements are not simply building blocks, like the particles studied by physicists. When the body's aggregates are attached to the elements, the body exists as a living, breathing being. Perhaps an example will help clarify this point.

Suppose a butcher kills a pig and cuts it up into four parts. When he sells the meat, the butcher no longer has the concept of pig. He is simply selling pork—ham or bacon or butt or some other part. Before the pig became pork, it was a living being with form, feelings, perceptions, perhaps some thoughts, and consciousness. These aggregates were bound to the elements. But when the pig is no longer alive, just the four elements remain.

The same is true of human beings. In life, the aggregates are linked to the elements. Every activity—thinking, breathing, perceiving, willing, and becoming conscious of countless things—arises depending on the combination of aggregates and elements. The feelings, perceptions, thoughts, and consciousness of this life pass away with this body. Without these aggregates, the body is like a log or a rock. All that's left are the elements.

Thinking in this way, it is easy to see that there is no difference between the elements inside the body and those outside. Both are impermanent, suffering, and without self. Let's look more closely at the four elements to help us develop deeper mindfulness of the body and its processes.

Earth. The earth element occupies space. It is hard or soft. It can expand and contract. It is visible, tangible, and perceptible. It has shape, size, and color. That is all we can know of the earth element. Although we can see a body, we cannot see the earth element separately within that body.

Like all elements, the earth element is impermanent. No matter how large, strong, colorful, or powerful it is, the earth element is always changing. There is no way to stop this natural process. However, nobody can make the earth element disappear. Consider planet Earth: We may urinate on it, defecate on it, spit on it, dig into it, throw trash on it, or clean it. Still, the earth element is neither disappointed with us nor pleased with us. It goes on changing in its own way, in its own time, unconcerned about what we do to it. We should, however, emulate the earth element in one important way: we should be as firm as earth in our determination to develop mindfulness.

When we meditate mindfully on the earth element in connection with one of the parts of the body, we feel the touch of hardness or softness, expansion or contraction. This feeling can be pleasant, painful, or neutral. As we pay attention to a particular sensation, it fades away, and another feeling arises. This process repeats again and again. If we don't identify with any of these feelings, they pass away, leaving simple awareness. We are quiet and peaceful without emotional reactions. We have equanimity.

Water. The water element is liquid and soft. It flows downward. Every part of the body needs water to survive, as do all living things. Water is characterized by cohesion. Powdery substances like cement and sand will not stick together unless water is added. Because of this quality, the water element in the body cannot be separated totally from other elements. When water predominates in one part, we say that it belongs to the water element, but saliva, blood, and other liquid parts of the body contain the earth, heat, and air elements as well.

Water is powerful enough to wash away cities and penetrate even the strongest rocks. When this power is harnessed, it can cut through steel and produce electricity. We emulate the water element when we harness our concentration to penetrate a meditation subject, such as a part of the body, and recognize its impermanence, suffering, and selflessness. Water also washes away impurities, just as meditation cleans and purifies the mind. But the flow of water can also be soft and gentle. When we meditate, we should be as flexible as water to adapt to the environment without complaints, and flow with people and situations without friction—without compromising our moral, ethical principles and mindfulness to blend with people who are immoral, unethical, and unmindful.

When we meditate mindfully on the water element, we feel the moisture that has penetrated the earth element. This feeling can be pleasant, painful, or neutral. If we do not identify with them, these feelings fade away. We remain in a quiet and peaceful state of equanimity without emotional reactions.

Heat. Though none of the thirty-two body parts belongs to the heat element, the body needs the right proportion of heat to maintain good health. Heat digests our food, maintains body temperature, and causes the body to grow. We experience the heat element when we feel warmth, radiation, or a burning sensation in some part of the body.

Heat is extremely useful. We use fire to cook and to warm our homes. Fire also burns garbage and other unnecessary stuff, just as we use meditation to burn impurities in the mind. Fire can also be dangerous and destructive. It keeps burning until it reduces things to ashes. We put out a dangerous external fire with water. Similarly, when the internal fire of greed, lust, or anger threatens to destroy our peace of mind, we use mindfulness and concentration to extinguish it.

When we meditate on the heat element, we feel the touch of gentle heat, too much heat, or neither. This feeling can be pleasant, painful, or neutral. If we don't identify with these feelings, they pass away, leaving us with awareness, peace, and equanimity.

Air. The function of the body's air element is oscillation and movement. Air occupies any space in the body. It moves in and out of the nostrils as we breathe; it moves within the lungs, stomach, and intestines; it circulates blood and other substances; it exits the body when we burp or expel gas.

The external air element is very useful. It cools the body like a gentle breeze and blows away dust. When the Buddha was surveying the world for people to listen to his teachings, he thought, "There must be some people who have a little dust in their eyes. By getting in touch with the cool air of Dhamma, they would wipe the dust from their eyes and see the truth." We meditate with the aim of blowing away the dust of mental impurities. As the Buddha said to his son Rahula, "Meditate like air."

When we meditate mindfully on the air element, we feel the touch of gentle air, too much air, or neither. This feeling can be pleasant, painful, or neutral. As we pay attention to the particular feeling, we notice it fading away. Then another feeling arises. If we do not identify with any of these feelings, they pass away, leaving us to awareness and equanimity. We remain quiet and peaceful.

When we meditate on the thirty-two parts of the body, we consider as well their connections to the four elements. For instance, we recall that blood cleans the body of wastes because it flows like water and moves like air. As we meditate on the parts and elements, we keep in mind that every part and element is impermanent, unsatisfactory, and selfless. As the Buddha said in his sutta on the elements:

> Bhikkhu, "I am" is a conceiving; "I am this" is a conceiving; "I shall be" is a conceiving; "I shall not be" is a conceiving; "I shall be possessed of form" is a conceiving; "I shall be form-less" is a conceiving. . . . By overcoming all conceptions, bhikkhu, one is called a sage at peace. And the sage at peace is not born, does not age, does not die; he is not shaken and is not agitated. For there is nothing present in him by which he might be born. Not being born, how could he age? Not aging, how could he die? Not dying, how could he be shaken? Not being shaken, why should he be agitated?

Deep awareness of this truth ends our suffering.

5: *Death and Impermanence*

Once the Buddha was speaking with his disciple Ananda about the causes of death.

The Buddha asked, "If there were absolutely no births of any kind anywhere—that is, of gods into the state of gods, of celestials into the state of celestials, of spirits, demons, human beings, quadrupeds, winged creatures, and reptiles each into their own state—if there were no births of beings of any sort into any state, then, in the complete absence of birth, would we discern aging and death?"

"Certainly not, venerable sir," Ananda replied.

"Therefore, Ananda, it is clear that there is one cause, source, origin, and condition for aging and death. Namely, birth!"

(tr. Bhikkhu Bodhi)

WE ARE BORN to die. Aging and death are our birthday gifts. As the Buddha taught, the cause of death is very simple . . . it is birth! We don't need to search for any other cause, since we are living with that cause within us. We cultivate mindfulness of death and impermanence so that we can accept this reality as it is.

Accepting the inevitability of death is healthier emotionally and spiritually than living in delusion. The Buddha said, "Beings who are subject to death often wish, 'May death never come to me!'" But wishing for life cannot stop death. Since this is so, the Buddha taught us to meditate on death—and even to use a corpse as an object of contemplation—to train us to face our own mortality without fear or superstition.

It is said that if there were a world in which people live for a thousand years, a Buddha would not appear in that world, because its people would not grasp the meaning of impermanence. Even in our own world, in which only a few people live for a hundred years, it is difficult to be mindful that death is inevitable. A man who lives to a ripe old age in good health may become proud of his longevity and forget his mortal nature. But if he is mindful of the certainty of death, he will be less arrogant and find it easier to forgive other peoples' mistakes.

We should not wait until old age or until we find out that death is approaching to get ready. Practicing mindfulness of death is the best way to overcome fear and prepare for a peaceful death. In fact, mindfulness is the only way death can be defeated, as the sutta says:

> Mindfulness is the path to the deathless,
> Negligence is the path to death.
> The mindful do not die,
> The negligent are dead already.

THREE KINDS OF DEATH

Everything that comes into existence because of causes and conditions is impermanent. Since we are born as a result of causes and conditions, we are also impermanent. When we understand impermanence well, we understand death well. As we have discussed, everything that exists has three moments: a rising moment, a living or peaking moment, and a moment of cessation. Every cell of our physical body, every feeling, perception, thought, and even consciousness itself, arises, reaches maturity, and then passes away. This is the nature of all conditioned things.

The Buddha taught us to distinguish three kinds of death: momentary death, conventional death, and eternal death. *Momentary death* is the kind of death that is occurring every moment. For instance, the physical cells that make up the body are always dying. Biologists tell us our bones produce 2.5 million red blood cells every second to replace dying cells. At the same time, our feelings, perceptions, thoughts, and consciousness are also dying, and new feelings, perceptions, thoughts, and consciousness arise to take their place. Mental processes change even more rapidly than cells and other physical things. We practice mindfulness to train ourselves to experience these inconceivably rapid mental changes.

By contrast, we become aware of the signs of decay of the physical parts of the body only through the marks they leave behind. When a storm is over, we see that trees are down, buildings have collapsed, and water is running everywhere. In the same way, aging reveals itself on the body through wrinkles, loss of teeth, hunched back, slow walk, slow talk, dry throat, weak sight, inability to taste, poor hearing, poor appetite, and gray hair. When we see these changes over time, we recognize that we are born with a one-way ticket!

When this process of aging ends, we experience *conventional death*. Normally this kind is what people have in mind when they say the word "death." But conventional death is just the doorway to a new life. Countless times we face conventional death, and countless times we take rebirth. A full cycle of momentary deaths and rebirths leading to conventional death is called one life. Another such series is called another life. This repeating pattern causes us to suffer tremendously. The goal of Buddhist practice is to end this cycle once and for all.

This ending is called *eternal death*. Both momentary death and conventional death are temporary. Both open a space and time for another birth. Again we have to go through the process of suffering—losing family and friends, growing old, facing death. But once we die the eternal death, our suffering dies forever. We do not have to endure another cycle of death and rebirth. Every death is a type of cessation, but eternal death is cessation with no further rebirth or what can be called cessation never to arise again. This cessation is nibbana, liberation, freedom from suffering. Nibbana is peace.

My Near-Death Experiences

Every night when I go to bed I think, "Tonight in my sleep, I may die." That idea never bothers me, because I have spent the day doing Dhamma work. I am happy to die with the satisfaction of a day's good work. I have also had several near-death experiences. They taught me what death means and how it happens. This knowledge helped me overcome any fear of dying.

Several times when I was young I nearly drowned. When I was in primary school, my brother and I had to cross a little creek between our home and the school. Neither of us knew how to swim. My mother was petrified we would drown there. Every day, when she heard the school bell, she would stand in the doorway of our house and wait for us. She knew what a magnet the creek was and how my brother and I longed to throw down our books, tear off our sarongs, and jump into the cool water.

Some days, we did. My mother, ever vigilant, would scream at the top of her lungs, and we would climb out reluctantly. Once, though, we got away with it. Mother did not see us when we jumped into the water. Right away, I was trapped in a small whirlpool where the stream flowed under a stand of bamboo. I flailed my arms to stay afloat, but the eddy sucked me down with terrifying force. Somehow my brother managed to pull me out.

When I was a little older, another brother saved me from drowning in an irrigation creek that had been swollen by monsoon rains into a small river. We never told our parents; we feared what would happen if we did. But my most serious near drowning happened in 1945 when I was almost eighteen.

I was waiting for a train that would carry me to a school for young monks. A novice monk, maybe eight or nine years old, invited me go swimming in the river near the station. Although I knew that I could not swim, how could I say no to this little novice? The novice tightened his under robe and jumped into the river. After swimming across, he saw me standing on the bank. "Jump," he shouted. Swallowing my embarrassment, I tightened my under robe and jumped. Almost immediately, I realized that I had made a big mistake. I struggled for a few moments. Then I sank to the muddy bottom, drinking in lots of filthy water.

When the novice realized I could not swim, he swam back and tried to hold up my head. But he was too small to pull me out. I panicked and grabbed his under robe. Naked, he swam to the shallow water and shouted for help. A man jumped into the river right through the window of a restaurant! The novice shouted that I might be dead already, but pointed to the place where he had last seen me .

Meanwhile, I had gone down three times. The last time I bobbed to the surface, I saw the entire world like a red ball. When I went down for the last time, I remember squatting on the river bottom. Suddenly, I saw a man bending over my body. I thought, "What is he doing? I was swimming." When I opened my eyes, the man stopped giving me mouth-to-mouth resuscitation, smiled, and moved away. Then I saw hundreds of people around me who had come to see my swimming adventure.

To this day, though I have traveled all over the world and crossed oceans countless times, I am uncomfortable around bodies of water! But these experiences and several other close brushes with death later in life have taught me not to be afraid. Having done my best to live by the principles the Buddha taught, I simply say to myself, "I have done what I could in my life."

Every day when I practice mindfulness meditation, I reflect on the impermanence of everything. This thought makes me feel very peaceful. In my view, this is how we all should die, with the knowledge that everything—including me—is always changing, disappearing, dying.

PREPARING FOR DEATH

Each day when we sit down to meditate, we should reflect on death as a part of our practice of mindfulness of the body. Contemplating death's inevitability is a good way for us to prepare for a peaceful death and fortunate rebirth. We remember that life is short, that death is certain, and that we cannot predict when this life will end. Doing so encourages us to practice generosity and loving-friendliness, strengthens our dedication to our practice, and arouses feelings of spiritual urgency.

When we meditate on death, we say to ourselves words such as the following:

> Perhaps tomorrow I will die. All those who lived in the past are dead, all those who are now living are dying, and all those who will come into existence in the future will die, without any exceptions. There is no certainty that I will live to finish such and such a project or until such and such a date. Before I die, I must overcome my greed, disappointment, anger, fear, jealousy, restlessness, worry, sleepiness, conceit, deceptiveness, wish for false reputation, and other deluded states of mind.
>
> The Buddha managed to defeat these inner obstacles. But even the Buddha, who attained full enlightenment, eventually succumbed to death. Only by understanding this point deeply and remembering it every day will I gain the courage to face death.

We can also reflect on these short sayings of the Buddha as part of our meditation:

> "Death always comes along together with birth."

"Just as people who have achieved great success in the world have died, so, too, I must certainly die."

"I who am dying moment after moment can die in the blink of an eye."

"The life of mortals is signless; its length cannot be known in advance."

"As fruit, when ripe, has to fall, as a potter's earthen jars eventually must all break up, so, too, does the life of mortals eventually come to an end."

"Not the least bit stoppable, always going forward, life rushes toward its end like the rising sun to its setting."

CEMETERY CONTEMPLATION

Another important aspect of preparing for death is cultivating a realistic attitude. Traditional rituals to honor the dead are often based on fear and superstition or on attachment to the person who died. Superstitions are psychological and emotional outlets for our memories of a loved one who has passed away. Ancestor worship as practiced in many cultures likely originated from attachment. It is also possible to be attached to one's own dead body. Some people say, "I don't mind dying, but I am afraid of being buried or cremated." Because of fear, they leave elaborate instructions for what they want done to their body after death.

But strong attachment and superstitions make it hard for us to develop mindfulness of death and impermanence. Some people have told me that they find mindfulness of death very unpleasant and wish to skip this part of the meditation. They don't want to think that worms eat the decomposed bodies of their loved ones. But according to

Theravada tradition, after the feelings, heat, and consciousness have left, a dead body is like a log. Practically speaking, it is worse than a log. At least a log can be used for fuel! Perhaps when its life force is gone, this body is useful only to medical students who can cut it up to gain knowledge about human diseases.

Perhaps one reason for our fear and superstition is that few people these days are lucky enough to see a dead body. Even if there is an opportunity, some people don't take it. They give orders to undertakers to do whatever they want with their dear ones' bodies. They say, "I don't want to look at the body of my mother or father. I want to remember my loved ones as they were, alive in good health." All they do is pay the undertakers' bills. That, in sense, is a kind of superstition.

Actually, at the time of the Buddha, people wrapped dead bodies in a white cloth and deposited them unburied in an outdoor area so that animals could eat them. They wanted even their dead bodies to be of some use to living beings. Monks were instructed to go to these places and collect the shrouds in which corpses had been wrapped. The Buddha's own robe was made of shrouds collected from the cemetery. In addition, after they gained full understanding of mindfulness of the body, the Buddha instructed his monks to contemplate the corpse as an object of meditation. This practice is called cemetery meditation. It is the best way to overcome superstitions about death.

Though we may not be able watch dead bodies decay as was possible during the Buddha's lifetime, we can use our imagination to contemplate what happens to a body after death. Meditating on this subject is not meant to encourage sadness or other negative emotions. Rather, it is the most realistic way to develop mindfulness of the body's impermanence. However, meditation on the various stages of a corpse requires spiritual maturity and emotional stability.

Once you have meditated thoroughly on the other aspects of mindfulness of the body, you may be ready to practice cemetery contemplation. First, imagine a dead body in the cemetery, one, two, or three days after death. Then compare your living body with that body with thoughts such as these:

> This is the nature of my body. It will become like this dead body. This result is unavoidable. Two, three, or four days after death, my body is bloated, discolored, festered, stinky. It has no feelings, perceptions, or thoughts. It rots. Animals eat it. The flesh disappears; the blood dries out; sinews break down; the bones separate. Bones also decay. They become porous and slowly are reduced to powder and dust. One day, when a big gust of wind blows, even this dust will disappear.

We can also reflect on these short sayings of the Buddha as part of our meditation:

> "When vitality, heat, and consciousness depart from this physical body, then it lies there cast away, food for others, without volition."

> "Before long this body will lie cast away upon the ground, bereft of all consciousness, like a useless block of wood."

KEY POINTS FOR MINDFULNESS OF DEATH

▸ The Buddha provided many examples to help you remember that life is short, death is inevitable, and the time of death is uncertain. For instance, he said, life is "like a flame blown out by the wind," "like lightening, a bubble, dew drops, or a line drawn in the water." Meditating on these examples helps to develop mindfulness of death.

▸ Also keep in mind that no man or woman who has ever lived, no matter how successful, famous, powerful, or holy, has escaped death. Even the Buddha died.

▶ Recall as well that the cause of death is birth and that the moment you were born, you begin to die.

▶ The countless momentary deaths of this life lead inevitably to conventional death. Nothing you do can prevent death from happening.

▶ Using meditation to develop mindfulness of the impermanence of all things, including your body, feelings, thoughts, perceptions, and consciousness, helps you to think realistically about death.

▶ Mindfulness of death arouses feelings of spiritual urgency and is the best way to prepare for a peaceful death and a fortunate rebirth.

▶ Superstitious attachment to a dead body makes no sense. Mindfulness of death can help you overcome superstitions.

▶ If you have meditated thoroughly on other aspects of mindfulness of the body—breath, four postures, clear comprehension, thirty-two parts, and four elements—and you are emotionally stable and spiritually mature, you should meditate on the stages of the corpse.

PART II:

Mindfulness of Feelings

6: *Sensations and Emotions*

Burdened with years, the householder Nakulapita went to see the Buddha. He said, "I am aged, venerable sir, come to the last stage, afflicted in body, often ill. Let the Blessed One instruct me."

"So it is, householder," the Buddha replied. "If anyone carrying around this body of yours were to claim to be healthy even for a moment, what is that other than foolishness? You should train yourself thus: 'Even though I am afflicted in body, my mind will not be afflicted.'"

Nakulapita delighted in the Blessed One's words. He paid respect to the Buddha and left. Then he approached the Venerable Sariputta and asked him to explain in detail the meaning of the Buddha's brief statement.

Venerable Sariputta said, "A person who is unfamiliar with the teaching of the Buddha regards the five aggregates as his self. With the change and decay of these aggregates, there arises in him sorrow, lamentation, pain, grief, and despair. Thus, he is afflicted both in body and in mind.

"A noble disciple who has heard the Dhamma, on the other hand, does not regard the aggregates as his self. The aggregates may change, but sorrow, lamentation, pain, grief, and despair do not arise in him. Thus, though he may still be afflicted in body, he is not afflicted in mind."

Nakulapita rejoiced, since this wise advice would lead to his welfare and happiness for a long time.

WE CAN SAY that the entire teaching of the Buddha is based on feelings. Toward the end of his life, after forty-five years of teaching, the Buddha said, "Bhikkhus, I have taught only two things:

suffering and the end of suffering." The story of Nakulapita points to the essence of the Buddha's teaching on ending the feeling of suffering. Because of our untrained body, senses, and consciousness, we suffer physical pain, such as that caused by illness and aging, and emotional pain, such as sorrow and grief.

Our suffering arises, as Venerable Sariputta explained to Nakulapita, because we regard the five aggregates—body, feelings, perceptions, thoughts, and consciousness—as being in our self or our self as being in them. In fact, the feeling we all have of *"I am"* or *"I exist"*—what Western psychology calls the "ego"—arises from clinging to these aggregates and regarding them as *mine* or *me*.

But through training in the second foundation of mindfulness—mindfulness of feelings—we can train our minds to use life's inevitable pains, such as illness and aging, as objects of meditation. However, we should not wait till we become old and ill like Nakulapita. If we build the habit now, when we experience painful feelings, we will understand that, like everything else, pain is impermanent. Moreover, there is no permanent self or *me* who is experiencing the pain! When we develop spiritually and realize this truth, neither physical pain nor mental unhappiness can cause us to suffer.

As we begin work on developing mindfulness of feelings, we should keep two points in mind. First, in English, we use the word "feeling" in two ways. It means both physical sensations that arise as a result of contact with external objects and inwardly generated emotions that are primarily mental or psychological. But in the Buddha's teaching, the word "feeling" (*vedana* in Pali and Sanskrit) includes both physical sensations and mental emotions. For clarity, I use the word "sensations" to refer to feelings that arise from external sensory contact and "emotions" to refer to non-sensory feelings that are generated internally. When I use the word "feelings," I mean to include both sensations and emotions.

Second, we must recognize that pain, sadness, and other unpleasant sensations and emotions are not the only feelings that cause us to suffer.

Pleasurable feelings, such as attachment, desire, and clinging, also cause suffering. As the *Dhammapada* says: "As a great flood carries away a sleeping village, so death seizes and carries away the man with a clinging mind, doting on his children and cattle." Clinging to anything—children, cattle, or really any persons, places, sounds, smells, tastes, touches, or ideas—is like sleeping. When we are attached, even pleasantly so, we are not mindful, and thus we are vulnerable to suffering. When we are free from desire, although the entire universe continues to change, we do not suffer.

THREE KINDS OF FEELINGS

The first step in developing mindfulness of feelings is distinguishing among the various kinds. Sometimes the Buddha says that there are two kinds of feelings—pleasant and unpleasant. Other times, he mentions three kinds—pleasant, unpleasant, and neutral. Neutral feelings are neither pleasant nor unpleasant.

When we have a pleasant feeling, we should be mindful that we are having a pleasant feeling. That's pretty straightforward. Whenever we feel pleasure, we know that it is pleasure. Similarly when we have a painful feeling, we know that it is painful feeling and can be mindful of that. People understand pleasant and unpleasant feelings naturally without too much explanation. The third category, neutral feelings, may be slightly more confusing for people who do not pay much attention to feelings. It helps to remember that in the Dhamma, there is no category called "mixed feeling."

Maintaining mindfulness of the three kinds of feelings is relatively easy, because when we pay attention, we notice that when we are experiencing a pleasant feeling, no unpleasant or neutral feeling is present. The same is true of an unpleasant and a neutral feeling. In other words, we experience one emotion or sensation at a time.

Moreover, when we are mindful, we notice very quickly that our feelings are always changing without any conscious control. Say, for instance, we are in a happy mood. The sun is shining, and we've finished our work and are heading home to a good dinner. But after a while, even though we might wish to hold on to that pleasant feeling, it disappears and a neutral feeling arises. Then, perhaps, we recall an argument we had with a friend during the day, and our neutral feeling changes to an unpleasant one. So from our experience we know very well that every feeling—pleasant, painful, or neutral—is impermanent.

Watching how quickly our feelings change, without any effort on our part, we realize another important truth. We begin to see that feelings are just feelings, not *my* feelings or parts of *me*. We realize that we often identify so closely with our feelings that they seem to be part of our basic identity. We say, *"My* knee hurts whenever *I* sit down to meditate" or *"I* am angry about the government," as if these feelings were unchanging parts of a self that is also permanent, everlasting, and immutable. But if our feelings were identical with the self, and the self were permanent, then our feelings of pain or anger should also be permanent. Experience tells us that this is not the case. Feelings change and our so-called self has no control over the changes. Observing this, we see very clearly that the self cannot be a permanent entity.

DEALING WITH PAIN

Of the three basic kinds of feelings we have been discussing—pleasant, unpleasant, and neutral—the unpleasant feeling of pain is likely the most difficult for us to manage. So long as we have a body and consciousness, we have pain. Even enlightened beings have pain. Once Devadatta, the Buddha's enemy, hurled a rock at the Buddha. A splinter hit the Buddha's foot. His personal physician, Jivaka, applied some medicine to the spot where the Buddha had bruises. That night the Buddha experienced excruciating pain. But using mindfulness, he endured the pain.

Unlike the Buddha, when painful sensations arise, we often become anxious, angry, or depressed. We react this way because we don't know how to deal with pain. The Buddha's basic instruction to his monks is very clear on this point: "When [a monk] is feeling a painful feeling, he becomes mindful that he is feeling a painful feeling." So the first step is simply to notice that we are feeling pain. But this instruction also tells us that the sensation of pain has both a physical and a psychological dimension.

Physical pain can often be overcome by medical treatment. So, of course, first we should do whatever we can to alleviate the pain, such as consulting a doctor or taking medicine. However, some ailments cause pain that persists no matter how much medicine we take. In such cases, we should follow the Buddha's example and use the pain as an object of meditation.

When we mindfully pay attention to a sensation of pain, the first thing we notice is that the sensation is always changing. For instance, a sharp stabbing pain changes to tingling pain, which changes to burning pain. In other words, like all feelings, pain is impermanent. As we become absorbed in watching these changing sensations, we start to relax and drop our resistance to the pain. As the barrier between *me* and the pain dissolves, and we watch the sensations ebb and flow, we may be surprised to observe that we are no longer suffering. The pain may still be there as a flow of sensations, but the *me* that was being hurt by the pain has disappeared!

The same technique can be used to deal with painful emotions, such as sadness, grief, or depression. When painful emotions arise, we pay attention to them. We notice that they are always changing. We watch them ebb and flow. For instance, we mindfully pay attention as grief changes to anger and then to anxiety or depression. We keep in mind that no permanently existing self is experiencing these emotions and that no painful emotion is permanent. This recognition in itself brings a measure of relief.

MANY KINDS OF FEELINGS

Once we understand the three basic kinds of feeling, we can begin to make more detailed distinctions. For instance, we are all familiar with pleasant and unpleasant feelings that arise through our five senses, such as the pleasant agreeable form of a beautiful flower or the unpleasant disagreeable smell of garbage. As the Buddha explained, when we consider the five types of sense consciousness and the objects they perceive—eyes and forms, nose and smells, ears and sounds, tongue and tastes, and skin and touches—we can distinguish fifteen types of feelings: pleasant, unpleasant, and neutral feelings linked to each sense.

We can also add a sixth sense, mind and mental objects such as thoughts, memories, imaginings, and daydreams. These can also be pleasant, unpleasant, or neutral. So now we have eighteen kinds of feelings. When we consider that each of these eighteen kinds can arise as either a physical sensation or an internally generated emotion, we have thirty-six. Multiplying these thirty-six by past, present, and future, we can distinguish 108 kinds of feelings!

You may be wondering, "What's the point of all these categories?" To answer this question, we remember that the Buddha's basic instruction on mindfulness of feelings is "contemplate the feeling in feelings . . . in order to know feelings as they really are." The Dhamma teaches us about 108 kinds of feelings to underscore that there are, indeed, many different kinds of "feeling in feelings."

In addition, when we start paying attention to feelings, at first we notice them only superficially. We practice being mindful of experiencing pleasant, unpleasant, and neutral feelings. As our mindfulness deepens, we begin to make further distinctions. So, for instance, we are mindful of the difference between sensations and emotions and of which sense consciousness is linked to the feeling. Only through practice can we distinguish among all 108 categories.

How Feelings Arise

So how do feelings arise? Understanding a little bit about this process helps us to develop mindfulness because we see that even a simple feeling, such as our pleasure when we see the form of a beautiful flower, arises from a series of interdependent steps. In brief, feelings arise dependent upon contact. Contact arises dependent on three other factors—the senses, an object, and consciousness. Here is how the process works:

Things that can be known by the mind through the senses, like a flower, are called mental objects. Each object has a certain quality or function. The senses are like the tentacles of an octopus. The tentacles make initial contact with the object and pass this contact along to the mind. However, the real contact takes place in the mind. Simultaneously with the exposure of the senses to an object, consciousness arises. The mind must be conscious to receive the contact passed along by the senses and interpret it correctly.

When the mind contacts an object, a mental impression arises in the mind that brings out the function of the object. This impression is feeling. Feeling can be compared to a hand that squeezes an orange to get orange juice. When pleasure is squeezed out of the object, we experience a pleasant feeling. When pain is squeezed out of the object, we experience an unpleasant feeling. This feeling can be either a physical sensation or a mental emotion.

The intensity and clarity of a particular feeling depends on many conditions. For example, if our eyes are healthy, the beautiful flower we are looking at is illuminated by bright sunlight, and we are standing close by and paying attention, our visual contact with the flower will be sharp and clear. As a result, the pleasant feeling arising from the eye contact will also be sharp and clear. But if our eyesight is poor, the light is dim, we are far away, or our consciousness is distracted, the flower will not make strong contact. In that case, the feeling that arises dependent on these conditions will be weak and subtle. The same applies to the other external senses.

In the same way, if the mind is clear, the thoughts arising in the mind are clear, and the feeling arising from the mind contact is strong. The feeling we get also depends on our mental state. An object may generate a pleasant feeling in one person and an unpleasant feeling in someone else, depending on the person's state of mind.

MEDITATING ON MINDFULNESS OF FEELINGS

When we meditate on mindfulness of feelings, we keep in mind that feeling arises dependent upon contact. As contact changes, the feelings also change. When we experience a pleasant feeling, we think, "This is a pleasant feeling. It has arisen depending on these factors. When these factors disappear, this pleasant feeling will also disappear." We do the same for an unpleasant feeling or a neutral feeling. We don't do anything to control our feelings or make them change. We only notice that our feelings are changing. Each feeling arises due to causes and conditions and then slips away. The mind cannot hold on to what we are experiencing and naturally lets it go. What else can it do? Nothing!

As we observe this process, we should not try to put our feelings into words. Labeling our sensations and emotions can actually distort them or disguise them as something else. Each person's feelings of pain or pleasure are totally personal. Feelings cannot really be conveyed in words exactly as they were experienced. We simply let the breath flow in and out. We stay fully awake and alert, paying total attention to each feeling as it arises, peaks, and passes away.

As we meditate, certain special feelings may arise. One of these is called "spiritual urgency." We see clearly that pain arises and pain disappears; pleasure arises and pleasure disappears. As we watch this repeating pattern, an insight arises that as long as we take birth in any form, we will continue to suffer. This insight inspires us to accelerate our spiritual practice and find a way to end this vicious cycle of birth and death right now, once and for all.

We may also experience a special feeling of pleasure as we meditate that does not have an underlying tendency toward desire. Our body becomes calm, our mind becomes calm, and there is no agitation, no excitement. We experience very deep peace. This pleasurable feeling, arising from knowing that this pleasurable feeling and everything else is impermanent, unsatisfactory, and selfless, does not arouse any attachment. We simply experience it. We see the reality.

Key Points for Mindfulness of Feelings

► You can practice mindfulness of feelings within your regular meditation on mindfulness of breathing.

► When feelings arise, notice whether they are pleasant, unpleasant, or neutral. Watch as each feeling arises, peaks, and passes away. You do not need to do anything to control these feelings or make them change. Simply observe and then return your attention to the breath.

► When feelings arise, notice whether they are sensations that result from contact with an external object or emotions that arise internally. Watch as each arises, peaks, and passes away; then return your attention to the breath.

► As you observe your sensations, notice which sense and sense consciousness is the source of the sensation. For example, are you feeling warmth arising from the touch contact between your skin and the cushion, or the sound of a bird outside the window, or the smell of the soup cooking in the kitchen? Don't verbalize these sensations or try to label them. Simply notice that you are experiencing a sensation and then return your attention to the breath.

▸ For instance, say that the sensation is the agreeable sound of a bird. Pay attention only to the process that allows you to hear the sound— sound waves making contact with your ear and being transmitted to your brain, which analyzes the contact and give rise to a mental impression or feeling. Remind yourself, "This is a pleasant feeling. It has arisen depending on these factors. When these factors disappear, this pleasant feeling will also disappear." Return your attention to the breath.

▸ If a sensation of physical pain arises, watch how the sensation changes. Watch its intensity ebb and flow without rejecting or resisting it. Remember that pain is not a thing, but an event. Pain is impermanent. There is no permanent I who is experiencing this sensation.

▸ If you feel an internally generated emotion, notice it without value judgment. Don't help it, hinder it, or interfere with it in the slightest. Simply watch as the emotion rises, peaks, and passes away. Then return your attention to the breath.

▸ For instance, if you experience a pleasant fantasy while you are meditating, notice that you have been distracted by a fantasy, notice how strong it is and how long it lasts. Notice the mental state of desire that accompanies the fantasy. Watch as it passes away and return your attention to the breath.

7: Harmful and Beneficial Feelings

Once there was a Brahmin named Akkosana, a person of high rank and authority. He had a habit of getting angry with everyone, even for no reason. When Akkosana heard that the Buddha never got angry, he went to see the Buddha and abused him with insults.

The Buddha listened patiently and compassionately. Then he asked Akkosana, "Do you have friends or relatives?"

"Yes, I have many relatives and friends," Akkosana replied.

"Do you visit them periodically?" the Buddha asked.

"Of course. I visit them often," said Akkosana.

"Do you bring gifts for them when you visit?" the Buddha continued.

"Surely. I never go to see them without a gift."

Then the Buddha asked, "When you give them gifts, suppose they do not accept. What would you do with the gifts?"

"I would take them home and enjoy them with my family."

Then the Buddha said, "Similarly, friend, you gave me a gift of your insults and abuse. I do not accept it. It is all yours. Take it home and enjoy it with your family."

Akkosana was deeply embarrassed. He understood and admired the Buddha's advice.

As we have discussed, we experience 108 different kinds of feelings. Both sensory contact with external objects through the eyes, ears, nose, tongue, and body and non-sensory contact with internal objects within the mind give rise to sensations and emotions. These feelings can be pleasant, unpleasant, or neutral. Some depend on past contact; others on present contact; still others on imagination of future contact. Feelings can be intense and clear or weak and subtle.

As we improve our ability to recognize the variety of sensations and emotions within the aggregate of feelings, we can also become mindful of the habits or tendencies that are their underlying causes. Three are essential: Some pleasant feelings have greed, desire, or craving as their underlying tendency. Some unpleasant feelings have anger or hatred as their underlying tendency. And some neutral feelings are rooted in ignorance or confusion.

Feelings that are activated by any of these negative tendencies are called "worldly." Worldly feelings arise most often when we are engaged in everyday pursuits, such as seeking wealth, companionship, a better job, or more power and recognition. Becoming aware of our tendencies toward anger and attachment and using mindfulness to subdue these habits gives us the opportunity to experience "spiritual" feelings, such as letting go, spiritual urgency, and the special joy we experience when we meditate. As our mindfulness deepens, we enjoy spiritual pleasant feelings more frequently.

Overcoming our negative tendencies takes hard work! Like Akkosana, we may have the habit of getting angry, even when there is no reason. Akkosana's habit was so strong that if a man who had been wronged did not get angry, Akkosana would get angry because the man did not! However, like Akkosana, when we become aware that anger has become a habit, we're often embarrassed. Anger is an unpleasant emotion that feels awful. Though it may take effort to become mindful of our anger and learn to control it, it's relatively easy for us to see that anger is harmful.

Desire and craving are much more difficult to recognize and eliminate. Pleasure generally feels good and makes us feel happy. It's easy to wish to hold on to our good feelings. Our habit is to cling to the pleasure we have, to want more, and to want to experience the pleasure again in the future. However, as we all know very well, whenever we try to hold on to a pleasurable feeling, we end up disappointed. Though it's less easy to remember that desire is harmful, when we think carefully, we see that to end our suffering, we must end our craving.

The third tendency is delusion. Ordinarily, we experience this feeling as confusion with regard to our self and how we exist. Sometimes when we experience a feeling that is neither painful nor pleasurable, we grab on to it with the thought, "Aha, this is real. Let me hold on to it!" We believe that there must be something real and permanent called *I* or *me* that is experiencing this feeling. When we look for this eternal self, it seems to be identical with the five aggregates or within the five aggregates. Only wise and diligent mindfulness can root out this harmful misconception.

In regard to these three, the Buddha's instructions are clear:

> Bhikkhus, the underlying tendency to lust should be abandoned in regard to pleasant feeling. The underlying tendency to aversion should be abandoned in regard to painful feeling. The underlying tendency to ignorance [delusion] should be abandoned in regard to neither-painful-nor-pleasant feeling. When a bhikkhu has abandoned [these] underlying tendencies, then he is one who sees rightly. He . . . has made an end to suffering.
>
> (tr. Bhikkhu Bodhi)

Let's look more closely at these three harmful feelings so that we can recognize them when they arise. We also consider beneficial feelings, such as loving-friendliness, joy, and equanimity, that can help us to overcome them. Our aim is to strengthen our mindfulness of feelings so that we, too, can see rightly and end our suffering.

ANGER AND HATRED

Anger often starts with a feeling of annoyance or irritation. The trigger can be anything: a work colleague gets a promotion we feel we deserve, a friend makes an unkind remark, a neighbor forgets again to put out the trash. If we ignore these feelings, they can grow into resentment, contempt, even hatred. The underlying tendency of these feelings is aversion—the feeling of disliking something and wanting to be separated from it.

When we pay attention, we see how miserable anger makes us feel. Our mind is cloudy, and our thoughts are tangled. We feel restless and agitated. We lose our appetite and cannot appreciate anything pleasurable. When we burn with what the Buddha calls the "fire of hatred," we are like a pot of boiling water—all hot and confused. Even meditation makes us irritated!

To control anger, the first step is becoming aware of it. With practice, we can learn to recognize the signs and take action before our feelings escalate. As soon as we notice that we are getting angry, we pay total attention to the feeling without trying to justify it. Anger grows when we remember past events, dwell on present situations, and imagine what might happen in the future. Instead, we use what we have learned about mindfulness to put out the fire. We think, "Anger is an unpleasant feeling. It has arisen in dependence on causes and conditions. Everything is impermanent. When these factors disappear, this unpleasant feeling will also disappear."

Here are some other ways to use mindfulness to overcome anger.

KEY POINTS FOR DEALING WITH ANGER

▸ Practice mindfulness of breathing. Take a few deep breaths. Inhale, exhale, and count one. Repeat up to ten. Then do the same, counting down from ten to one. Continue until you feel calm.

▸ Practice restraint. If a conversation seems likely to become an argument, simply stop talking. During the pause, use mindfulness to investigate whether jealousy, stinginess, vengefulness, or some other unwholesome feeling is hiding behind your words. Practice patience to buy time so that you can say the right thing at the right time.

▸ Avoid blaming. When you say, "It is not my fault. He always does something to make me angry," you sound just like a child saying, "He started it!" Don't blame yourself, either. It takes two to have an argument.

▸ Talk to a warm-hearted friend. Your friend might remind you, "You cannot know what is going on in someone else's mind. There may be reasons for this behavior that you can't see."

▸ Cultivate gratitude. When you are angry, it is easy to forget the good things someone has done for you. Being grateful softens your heart.

▸ Practice generosity. Change the atmosphere between you and a person with whom you are angry by offering a gift or other favor. Doing so may give both of you a chance to apologize.

▸ Listen to the Dhamma. Find a Dhamma talk on the web or read a Dhamma article or book. Even if the subject does not pertain to anger, when you hear the Dhamma, your anger fades.

▸ Avoid angry people. Spending time with people prone to anger can make you tense and anxious. Eventually, you may become angry as well.

▸ Make a commitment. In the morning, when your mind is fresh, say words such as, "Something might happen today to make me angry. A conversation, a person, or a situation I cannot anticipate may irritate me. Whatever comes up, today I am going to do my best to be mindful and not get angry."

▶ Remember that you do want to die with anger. If your mind is confused at the time of death, you may be reborn in a painful state. Life
is short. Live yours in peace and harmony, without anger.

Using mindfulness in this way is a type of skillful effort. First, we
try to prevent anger from arising. If it does arise, we take steps to overcome it. These two activities work together to make us calm. One day
we will say, "Ah, it is wonderful. I am a different person now. I can han-
dle my anger. This has become possible because of my mindfulness."

When the mind is calm, it is easy to cultivate loving-friendliness
(*metta* in Pali and *maitri* in Sanskrit). This beneficial feeling is a natural
sense of interconnectedness with all beings. Because we want peace,
happiness, and joy, we know that all others—including anyone with
whom we have had difficulties—must also wish for these qualities. The
daily mindfulness practice I suggest on pp. 11–14 is a good way to begin.
Loving-friendliness heals the wounds of anger. We feel comfortable,
secure, and so relaxed that we can talk with anybody without getting
angry. Even if someone insults us, we respond with patience and compassion, as the Buddha did to Akkosana.

DESIRE AND CRAVING

Desire is everywhere. Every living thing has the desire to stay alive.
Even plants "strive" to propagate themselves. Craving is our creator.
Our parents' craving for each other and our craving for rebirth combined
to create us. Even painful feelings give rise to craving. When a painful
feeling arises, we do not like it. We wish to get rid of the pain, and we
wish to enjoy some pleasure. Both wishes are craving.

Surely, we think, desire is necessary. Without it, there would be no
birth. Life as we know it would end. In a way, we are right. Desire *is*
the underlying motivation for the continuation of life in samsara, the
cycle of uncontrolled death and rebirth. As the sutta tells us, "All dhammas converge in feeling."

Of course there are moments of pleasure or enjoyment in our life. We are not suffering all the time. Sixty such moments are mentioned in the Four Foundations of Mindfulness Sutta. Enjoyment is the reward we get for all this suffering. That is why we live. But we must work very hard to get this pleasure, because pain comes along with it. As our growing understanding of mindfulness teaches us, whenever we experience a pleasant feeling, we wish to hold on to it. If someone suggests that clinging is a problem, we get upset and try to justify it: "How can I live without clinging to my family, my house, my country?"

The truth is, we don't really want to be free from desire or to admit that clinging to the pleasures of the senses—the taste of delicious food; the sound of music, gossip, or a joke; the touch of a sexual embrace— ends unavoidably in disappointment and suffering. We don't have to deny that pleasant feelings are pleasurable. But we must remember that like every other feeling, pleasure is impermanent. Wishing to keep any person, place, possession, or experience with us forever is hopeless!

Moreover, the wish for sensory pleasure distracts us from our mindfulness. When we are sitting on the cushion, the desire might arise in us to eat a piece of chocolate or to feel the touch of our partner. If we allow this feeling to grow, our mindfulness vanishes. Desire takes over and we reflect: "This is a beautiful feeling. It gives me pleasure. This taste, smell, touch, or sound gives me pleasure . . . this is all I need in my life. It makes me happy, comfortable; it makes me healthy and strong. It gives me full satisfaction."

But then, perhaps, we recognize, "I have this desire in me." We remember that sensory pleasure binds us to this life and future lives. It disrupts our mindfulness and blocks our ability to attain higher states of concentration. What we really want is to enjoy the profound pleasure of deep meditation that leads to liberation from the cycle of suffering. When we are bound to sensory pleasure, liberation is impossible.

So we use mindfulness to penetrate the superficiality of our desire and reflect: "If I cling to this object, I will end up in pain. . . . I can't hold on to it forever; I have no way of controlling it. If I get involved in it, I'll lose my mindfulness. I have enjoyed many things in life . . . where are they now? Why should I sacrifice this precious moment for the sake of superficial satisfaction? . . . let me not think of it." Because of mindfulness, our desire fades away, at least for the moment. When it disappears, we notice that it is gone. We reflect, "That desire is no longer in my mind." We remain mindful to make sure that it does not come back.

Pleasure without pain is possible only as we progress toward higher states of mindfulness. Unlike sensory pleasure that leads only to an instant of temporary happiness, the joy we feel when we achieve deep concentration brings peace and tranquility. This beneficial feeling is accompanied by energy and focus, along with the wholesome desire to experience the wonderful feeling of joy again and again. (I explore this topic in much more detail in my book *Beyond Mindfulness in Plain English*.)

Delusion

Delusion is the confused way we regard all objects, including *me*, as permanent and as possessing a self or soul. Because of this confusion, we believe that objects and our feelings about them—pleasant, unpleasant, or neutral—can bring us permanent happiness or cause us permanent misery.

We often notice this confusion when we experience a neutral feeling. Even though we are healthy and have done our meditation as well as we can, we have some kind of nagging feeling in our mind. This feeling is neutral, neither pleasant nor unpleasant, but its underlying tendency is confusion. We think, "*I* exist. This is how my self works. This feeling and all other feelings are part of *me*."

What causes this confusion? For one thing, when we remember our childhood, we believe the same *I* existed then as now, ignoring the many ways our body, feelings, and other aggregates have changed since *I* was a child. We also believe that this same *I* will live into our old age and even into the next life, ignoring all of the changes that will happen between now and then.

The information we get from our senses seems to support this mistaken view. When we see our current body, hear our current voice, smell our current smell, taste food and drink, and touch physical objects, we think, "These are the senses that *I* had yesterday, last week, last month, eighty years ago. *I* still remember the conversation I had with him or with her. This same *I* existed then and will continue to exist through time."

But even a basic understanding of impermanence reveals that this belief is mistaken. All forms, feelings, perceptions, thoughts, and even consciousness itself are impermanent—arising, existing for a time, and then passing away. Happily, all of our confused habits of mind are also impermanent, even delusion itself. Like anger and craving, delusion arises dependent on causes and conditions. When these causes and conditions change, as they can as a result of our practice of mindfulness, delusion itself vanishes.

EQUANIMITY

The beneficial feeling we hope to cultivate through our mindfulness practice is equanimity. When we rest in equanimity, our feelings are in perfect balance. We neither push away unpleasant feelings nor grasp at pleasant ones. We are not confused by ignorance and see everything very clearly. Since we don't identify our self with our feelings, they pass quietly away, leaving us at peace. As a feeling, equanimity is both neutral and spiritual. It is neither pleasant, nor unpleasant, but it is not indifferent. We are awake and alert and can continue our observation of our body, feelings, thoughts, and other experiences without being pushed and pulled by desire or aversion.

As the sutta tells us, when we are in a state of equanimity and see a pleasant, unpleasant, or neutral sight, we recognize that it is conditioned, gross, and dependently arisen. Then we return to equanimity as quickly as we might open or shut our eyes. The same is true for each of the other senses:

> When [meditators] hear a pleasant, unpleasant, or neutral sound, they understand that it is conditioned, gross, and dependently arisen. Then they turn their minds to equanimity just as quickly as a man snaps his fingers.
>
> When they smell a pleasant, unpleasant, or neutral smell, they understand that it is conditioned, gross, and dependently arisen. Then they turn their minds to equanimity just as quickly as drops of water roll off a sloping lotus leaf. . . .
>
> Similarly, when they experience an idea with their minds and a pleasant, unpleasant, or neutral sensation arises, they understand that it is conditioned, gross, and dependently arisen. Then, just as when two or three drops of water fall onto an iron plate that has been heated for a whole day, the falling of the drops might be slow, but they quickly evaporate and disappear. In the same way sensations arisen due to ideas are replaced quickly and easily with equanimity.

With equanimity, we are no longer troubled by the ups and downs of pleasure and pain. Mind and body are in balance. We are free of restlessness, agitation, and worry. Confusion has ended and we rest in harmony with reality. Even the subtle desire for a beautiful experience to continue has disappeared. Instead, we feel immeasurable loving-friendliness and boundless compassion.

Having completely let go of what the Buddha calls "low quality" pleasant feelings—the pleasures of family, friends, good health, prosperity—we experience "high quality" pleasant feelings—the profound joys of higher states of meditative concentration. With each higher state, our enjoyment increases until we attain what the

Buddha calls "the cessation of feeling and perception." From there we can move to the highest quality pleasure of all, nibbana, total liberation from suffering.

PART III:

Mindfulness of Mind

8: *Mind and Consciousness*

The Buddha was explaining to his bhikkhus what he had done to overcome unwholesome thoughts that arose in his mind while he was still an unenlightened bodhisatta.

"It occurred to me," the Buddha said, "suppose I divide my thoughts into two classes. On one side, I set thoughts of sensual desire, ill will, and cruelty. On the other side, I set thoughts of renunciation, loving-friendliness, and compassion.

"As I abided thus, diligent, ardent, and resolute, a thought of sensual desire arose in me. When I considered that this thought leads to my own affliction and the affliction of others, it subsided in me. When I considered that this thought obstructs wisdom, causes difficulties, and leads away from nibbana, it subsided in me. Thus I abandoned it, did away with it, removed it. . . .

"Whatever a bhikkhu frequently thinks upon, that will become the inclination of his mind. If he ponders renunciation, if he has abandoned the thought of sensual desire to cultivate the thought of renunciation, then his mind inclines to thoughts of renunciation."

THESE WORDS, taken from the Two Kinds of Thought Sutta, illustrate the most important practical lesson in the Buddha's teachings on the third foundation of mindfulness, mindfulness of mind: whatever thoughts we cultivate frequently become a mental habit. Just as the Buddha abandoned thoughts of wishing for sensual pleasure by cultivating thoughts of renunciation, he did away with thoughts of anger by thinking of compassion and thoughts of cruelty by thinking of loving-friendliness. What simple good sense this advice is!

But the Buddha's advice goes one step further, as the sutta tells us. He also warned his monks that too much thinking—even beneficial thoughts such as renunciation, compassion, and loving-friendliness—tires the body and strains the mind. "When the mind is strained," the Buddha explained, "it is far from concentration." So rather than thinking at all, he "steadied his mind internally, quieted it, brought it to singleness, and concentrated it." "Meditate, bhikkhus," the Buddha concluded, "do not delay, or else you will regret it later." With this, "the bhikkhus were satisfied and delighted in the Blessed One's words."

As we work toward the state of single-pointed, concentrated meditation that the Buddha encourages in this sutta, we encounter a formidable obstacle—our own mind or consciousness. In Buddhist writings, the untamed mind is often described using animal metaphors. Sometimes it is a newly captured "wild elephant" that screams and tramples and pulls against the rope of mindfulness. Other times it is the "wandering monkey mind" that roams all over the universe through imagination. We have all experienced this mind. We are trying to meditate or even to fall asleep, but thoughts distract us. We remember injustices, wars, problems, places, situations, books we have read, people we met long ago, our job, house, family, friends, relatives, and many other things.

Clearly, we need more of the Buddha's good advice so that we can convince this monkey to settle down! As a first step, let's look more closely at what the Buddha says about the nature of mind so that we can move ahead with better understanding.

MIND OR CONSCIOUSNESS

So what is consciousness? Is it the same as mind? Where is it? And how does it function? These are difficult questions, but let's do our best to look at them in a way that helps to deepen our practice of mindfulness. As you already know, consciousness is one of the five aggregates, along with the body, feelings, perceptions, and thoughts. As is true of all the aggregates, consciousness is always changing. In fact, it changes much faster than anything else. Not knowing how consciousness arises, how it ends, and what leads to that end is called ignorance. That is why consciousness is so difficult to understand.

The function of the aggregate of consciousness is basic awareness. When we speak about this function, we sometimes use the word "mind." Mind is a non-physical phenomenon that perceives, thinks, recognizes, experiences, and reacts. It is clear and formless, which means that thoughts and other mind objects can arise in it. It is also described as luminous, which means "able to shine light on things"— in other words, "knowing."

There is no single place in the body where mind is stored. Some people say that the mind resides in the heart. The Pali word *citta* means both mind and heart. Others say that it exists in the brain. Still others believe that the mind is located all over the body and operates through the brain and central nervous system. The Buddha did not mention a particular place as the home of mind. He simply used the phrase "cave of the body."

Though consciousness is present in every thought, perception, and feeling, it does not have independent existence. In fact, we don't notice consciousness at all until it meets with an object. Consciousness arises dependent on the six senses and their contact with objects. It even has different names according to the sense through which it arises—sight consciousness, smell consciousness, touch consciousness, and so on. For instance, when the ear contacts the sound of a train whistle or a woman singing, sound consciousness arises. When the mind contacts internal objects, such as thoughts and memories, mind consciousness arises.

Thus, there is no such thing as mere mind or mere consciousness.

We know mind only by its contents. It is always hanging on to a thought, feeling, perception, the body, or some mental object. In itself, the consciousness that arises as a result of contact with objects is pure. But almost simultaneously with consciousness, desire ("I want this"), hatred ("I don't want that"), delusion ("This is me"), or some related confusion arises. The mind wants to shine by itself, but its mental contents don't allow it. They conceal the mind's luminosity and distort our ability to know things as they really are.

The best we can say is that mind is an impermanent and dependent phenomenon. It arises as a result of causes and conditions. Understood in this way, instead of the word "mind," it makes more sense to talk about the "body-mind complex"—the combination of mental factors (including contact, feeling, perception, attention, concentration, life force, and volition) that work together in each instant of consciousness.

Since consciousness arises as a result of causes and conditions, the consciousness of this life must also have come from causes and conditions.

So what is our role in this process? Did we select our present life? And can we choose where this stream of consciousness will arise next? Unfortunately, the answer to both questions is no, or at least, not directly.

As the Buddha has explained, at the time of death, we have already made all the arrangements for the next life—not by writing a will, but by engaging in countless actions of body, speech, and mind. These thoughts, words, and deeds are causes, the first half of the universal principle of cause and effect known as *kamma* (or karma). Our present life is the second half of the principle—the result of the causes we created in previous lives. Thus the consciousness that arises in this life can be called a stream of "result consciousness." Our kamma, combined with our craving for rebirth and our ignorance, propel us to start the process of birth, aging, and death all over again.

The kamma we have created determines the nature of our rebirth:

good actions lead to a fortunate rebirth; bad actions, to an unfortunate one.

Of course, the good news is that there is one thing we can do immediately to make sure that our next life is a fortunate one. Right now, while we are alive, we can use mindfulness to train ourselves to avoid thoughts, words, and deeds motivated by sensual desire, anger, cruelty, and other causes of bad kamma and to cultivate beneficial actions motivated by renunciation, compassion, loving-friendliness, and other causes of good kamma!

Cleansing the Mind

So how do we practice mindfulness of mind? Since we know mind only by its contents, we cannot contemplate or focus on just the mind. In a nutshell, the practice consists of cleansing the mind so that the harmful tendencies toward desire, hatred, and ignorance—the same tendencies that caused us to take rebirth—do not have the opportunity to manifest as actions. If they do arise, we make the effort to overcome them. And when they are overcome, we make the effort to replace them with beneficial states of mind.

Desire, hatred, delusion, and other poisons are able to pollute the mind because of the harmful tendencies or inclinations we created by our previous actions. As the Buddha explained in the Two Kinds of Thought Sutta mentioned at the beginning of this chapter, whatever thoughts we cultivate frequently become a habit. For instance, when we are accustomed to angry thoughts, it is easier to entertain angry thoughts in the future.

These harmful tendencies hide within the mind until they are activated by contact with external objects and situations. That's why, for example, spending time with angry people can activate our own tendency to anger. However, once the mind is purified, we no longer have to guard our senses against external situations that can stimulate deluded thoughts. A person who insults us does not make us angry; a person who craves wine and offers us some does not make us want to get drunk ourselves. As the sutta explains:

> As rain gets into an ill-thatched house, so craving gets into an untrained mind. As rain does not get into a well-thatched house, so craving does not get into a well-trained mind.

Worrying over or dwelling upon harmful actions we have done in the past is a waste of time and energy. Instead, we should put our efforts into cultivating beneficial thoughts to overcome and replace harmful ones. In fact, we must cultivate thoughts of generosity, compassion, loving-friendliness, and equanimity again and again in order to weaken and destroy harmful inclinations and create beneficial ones.

We do this most effectively by practicing mindfulness meditation. As I have mentioned, our practice consists of two types of meditation: concentration meditation or *samatha* and insight meditation or *vipassana*. Concentration meditation suppresses the hindrances and makes the mind calm, peaceful, and luminous. Hindrances are negative tendencies that obstruct our spiritual progress and interfere with our ability to concentrate. I explain more about the hindrances in chapter 10. Insight meditation, which we have been calling mindfulness, eradicates the hindrances and all other negative tendencies. It helps us to overcome ignorance so that we can be liberated from samsara, the cycle of repeated births and deaths.

Key Points for Practicing Mindfulness of Mind

▶ If you are sitting on your meditation cushion and a craving arises in your mind, like lust, what should you do? First, acknowledge that if there were no tendency toward craving in your mind, craving would have not arisen. Although your mind is luminous, it is not totally pure.

► Next, recognize the possibility of liberating your mind from craving. Observe your thoughts without following them until the craving thoughts fade away.

► When the craving ends, recognize that it has gone. You think, "This is wonderful! This mind was full of craving before. Now there is none. That means even I have the chance to liberate this mind from craving."

► Reflect on the nature of a craving-free mind. It is generous, gentle, compassionate, and happy to renounce thoughts of sensual pleasure. With this confidence you proceed.

► Another time, while you are meditating, you hear a sound. Somebody is walking loudly. Somebody coughs. Somebody sneezes. Somebody is snoring. And aversion or anger arises.

► You get irritated and begin to question: "Why doesn't this person walk quietly? Why doesn't this person take some cough medicine? Why doesn't this person stay in a cabin alone and meditate there without troubling us? Why doesn't the person sitting next to this snoring person wake him up?"

► These questions and many more thoughts bother you. You get angry. Hateful thought can arise in any of the four postures, sitting, standing, walking, or lying down.

► When hate arises, you recognize, "Hateful thoughts have arisen in me." Hate arises depending on previous experiences. It arises depending on causes or conditions. You cannot predict when hate will arise.

► So you use the techniques of mindfulness you have been practicing to overcome these thoughts. Pay attention to the thought without following it. Observe the impact of hatred on your consciousness.

Don't think of any incident, any situation, or any person. Don't verbalize by saying, "My mind is full of hatred." Words block awareness of what is going on in your mind. Just pay attention and recognize what has arisen as having arisen.

▸ Reflect on the nature of a hate-free mind. It is beautiful, peaceful, relaxed, and loving-friendly.

▸ Suddenly, thoughts of friendliness and compassion arise. These have no particular object and are focused on no particular person. Recognize them, feel them, delve into them, accept them—simply be with them.

▸ The mind must be free from delusion to understand that it is free from delusion. Before delusion arose in your mind, it was clear, just as before you fell asleep, you were awake. All you need do at that moment is to pay attention to the fact that your mind is clear.

▸ When you pay attention, the clouds of delusion slowly fade away and the clear blue sky-like mind appears again. You see that consciousness is always changing. Thoughts arise and disappear. They are impermanent. When delusion arises you pay attention to it, knowing that it is a delusion. Then it slowly fades away. Then you know mind as clear, aware, luminous.

9: *Mental States*

One day, someone brought a delicious dish of fish to offer to the monks at a temple. In that temple lived one monk and one temple boy. When the monk sat down to eat, the boy offered him the whole dish. In it were eight small pieces of fish. The monk took three at once.

As the monk ate, the temple boy watched attentively. He said to himself, "Well, he is the monk and the head of the temple. Let him have three pieces. There are five more. That is enough for my lunch and dinner."

When the monk finished eating, he stretched out his hand to pick up more fish.

The temple boy thought, "Surely, he is the monk and the head of the temple. He deserves half of this dish. Let him have one more."

This time the monk took two pieces.

Then the boy thought, "Never mind, let him have five pieces. There are three more. That is plenty for me."

After eating the two pieces, the monk helped himself to two more, leaving only one small piece of fish in the dish.

Then the boy thought, "Never mind. I am small. He is big. One piece is enough for me."

When the monk reached for the last piece, the boy's patience ran out. "Venerable sir," he cried. "Are you going to eat this last piece of fish without leaving anything for me?"

In his greed for fish, the monk was so unmindful that he had totally forgotten the faithful temple boy, waiting patiently to have his meal. The monk was so embarrassed that, ever after, he refrained from eating greedily.

D EVELOPING MINDFULNESS of greed and other states of mind is
hard work. As we have noted, because we see mind only by its
contents, we cannot contemplate the mind by itself. When consciousness with greed arises in the mind, instead of looking at the mind, we
quickly do what the greedy mind demands, as we see clearly in the traditional story of the greedy monk and the temple boy. We follow our
instinct, acting blindly and impulsively, even if we suspect we may
regret our actions later. Once the mind is obsessed, we seldom have
enough discipline to be mindful. We speak, think, and act in bewildered
haste.

Mindfulness training teaches us to pause and look at the mind. First,
we practice while sitting on the cushion. As thoughts come and go, we
watch them arise, peak, and pass away. Since we are not engaging in
immediate action based on our impulses, we are able to assess our mental states calmly. The Four Foundations of Mindfulness Sutta recommends that we watch particularly for eight pairs of mental states. Our
goal is learning to recognize whether the mind is:

1. greedy or not greedy,
2. hateful or not hateful,
3. deluded or not deluded,
4. contracted/distracted or not contracted/distracted,
5. not developed or developed,
6. not supreme or supreme,
7. not concentrated or concentrated,
8. not liberated or liberated.

The first four pairs of mental states can be experienced both during
meditation sessions and while we are engaging in everyday activities.
After practicing awareness of them on the cushion, we often find it
easier to be mindful of them at other times. The last four pairs focus
on states we achieve only through dedicated meditation practice.
Knowing about these states inspires us to try to attain them. To begin,
let's look briefly at each pair to help us recognize them.

Greedy or not. We have all acted on impulse like the greedy monk. Suppose we see a dish of food on a buffet table that we like very much. Our greedy mind becomes active. We scoop deeply into the dish and serve up a big portion without thinking about the people lined up behind us eyeing the same dish. The goal of mindfulness training is becoming aware of our mental states so that we can take steps to short-circuit our impulsive actions. The moment we realize that our mind is obsessed, we think about the discomfort we might cause others who are waiting their turn. Like the greedy monk in the story, we apply the discipline of mindfulness in a practical way to change our behavior.

When our greed disappears, even for a short period, we immediately feel more comfortable. We notice that easy state of mind and also recognize that greed can arise any time, any place, and in any situation. When we pay attention, we find many opportunities to reflect on our mental state and to practice self-control.

I walk as much as I can every day. Often I see deer that have been shot by hunters. Sometimes the hunters cannot find them, and the carcasses rot by the roadside. I also see trash thrown by the road—beer cans, liquor bottles, TV antennas, refrigerators, tables, and other household junk. Throughout the spring and summer, this garbage also rots.

Because I desire to see a clean environment, these sights sometimes disturb my mind. But then mindfulness intervenes. I remind myself that desire does me more harm than good. Even the wholesome wish for people to stop hunting or to dispose properly of their trash unsettles my mind and causes me to suffer. So, instead of being attached to my environmental principles, I remind myself that I cannot fix the whole world and let go of my desire. I may not be able to remove the world's greed, but I can get rid of my own. The moment I do, I begin to relax. Then and there I experience peace.

Hateful or not. In its natural state, the mind is like cool, calm, and clear water. Hateful thoughts overheat the mind. Under their influence, the mind boils like a pot of water, distorting our ability to think clearly or see things as they are. Our relaxed, calm, and peaceful state of mind dissolves, and the mind simmers with jealousy, vengefulness, malicious thoughts, thoughts of cruelty. We want to cause harm to someone. If we do not intervene with mindfulness, the mind orders the tongue to become active and we wound others with harsh words.

Mindfulness suffocates anger by taking away the fuel it needs to keep burning. When hate fills our mind, we should think: "Hate makes me sick. My thinking is confused. A sick mind defeats the purpose of my meditation. Only with a calm and peaceful mind can I see myself clearly and reach my goal." The Buddha described the relief we feel when we overcome hate-filled thoughts in this way:

> Suppose that a man were to become sick, afflicted, gravely ill, so that he could not enjoy his food and his strength declined. After some time, he recovered from that illness so that he could enjoy his food and regain his bodily strength. He would reflect on this, and as a result he would become glad and experience joy.

Deluded or not. Recognizing delusion is tricky. The mind must be free from delusion to understand that it is free from delusion! So how can we tell that we are deluded? The secret is remembering that, by nature, the mind is clear and luminous. We have experienced this clarity many times—perhaps during a peaceful session of meditation, or just before falling asleep, or when we first wake up in the morning. We should make a habit of noticing this clarity when it occurs. Then, when delusion arises, it is easier to recognize it.

Delusion most often manifests as confusion about who we are and how we exist. When strong greed or hatred grips the mind, we think, "I must have that" or "I despise that." The *I* that arises at that time feels very solid and very needy. It's as if the mind is locked in jail by that powerful need. We feel that if this need cannot be met, *I* will die! But, remember, before the mind was imprisoned, it was free. That memory of freedom helps us to become mindful.

The key is impermanence. When we pay attention to deluded thoughts, the cloud of confusion slowly fades. Soon the clear, blue sky-like mind appears again. When we recognize delusion as delusion, delusion ends—at least temporarily. When we attain the liberation of nibbana, freedom from delusion becomes permanent.

Contracted/distracted or not. A contracted mind is depressed or withdrawn. This mental state, related to displeasure, can occur at any time. Sometimes we experience it when we are sitting on the cushion and the thought arises that we are not making any progress in our meditation. We think, "Nothing works for me. Everyone else is happy and peaceful. I'm the only one who never gets it right!" This mind also shows up during ordinary activities. We think, "Nobody loves me. I am so old, so fat, so ugly. I always say the wrong thing, do the wrong thing."

When we become mindful that the mind is contracted in this way, the only thing to do is to keep watching and watching. Don't rationalize or justify. Don't allow one thought to lead to another. Don't hold on at all. Just pay attention. This state of mind is also impermanent. Like any other, it slowly fades away.

The opposite of a contracted mind is a distracted one. The mind expands beyond all boundaries. The whole universe seems open and welcoming. We feel that we are really someone special. This mental state is also an obstacle. If we don't rein it in with purposeful attention, it escapes like the "monkey mind" and travels all over the universe through imagination.

Not developed or developed. In everyday consciousness, we do not experience the developed mental state. Some translators use the word "exalted" to describe it. We reach this calm, peaceful, and tranquil state only as a result of deep concentration meditation. The mind has gone beyond normal consciousness. We feel as if we are floating a few feet above the ground. The mind is harmonious, relaxed, serene, bright, and balanced. Even accomplished meditators do not achieve this state every time they practice.

When the meditation session ends and the mind returns to normal awareness, we experience the mental state that is not developed. Our ordinary consciousness with its sense experiences returns. We become aware that the mind is not anything special.

Not supreme or supreme. The next pair of mental states also refers to the attainments of deep concentration meditation. "Supreme" means that we have reached "the highest state." After the Buddha became enlightened, he said that his mind had attained an unsurpassable, peerless, or transcendent state. An accomplished meditator can also achieve this kind of mental experience. The mind is pure, soft, steady, and imperturbable. Although it is wonderful, this state is temporary. Only when we achieve liberation does it become permanent. Any other mental state achieved during meditation is not supreme. This term acknowledges that we know that it is possible for us to achieve a state that is superior.

Not concentrated or concentrated. Sometimes when we meditate, the mind is able to concentrate on one thing without interruption. When we achieve this level of single-pointed focus, we train ourselves to be mindful of it, recognizing concentrated mind as concentrated mind. When the mind is contracted or distracted, we recognize that our mental state is not concentrated.

Sometimes when people have distracted mind, rather than cultivating simple awareness, they complain, "My mind is jumping all over the place. I can't concentrate." Thinking along these lines leads only to more grumbling and more worry. Instead, we should follow the Buddha's advice and simply notice. Soon, the mind that is not concentrated fades and it becomes possible to achieve concentration once again. The key is observing with mindfulness.

Not liberated or liberated. A liberated mind is free of all problems. It is not greedy, hateful, deluded, contracted, or distracted. It is developed, supreme, and concentrated. In the highest states of concentration meditation, it is possible to achieve temporary liberation. But even temporary liberation from harmful mental states is an extraordinarily beneficial experience. If we follow the steps of mindfulness very closely, eventually the mind may become fully liberated.

Working with Mental States

The pairs of mental states we have been considering do not always arise in the mind in the order given in the sutta. However, it is certain that when one half of a pair is present in consciousness, the other half is not. So, for instance, when greed fades away, we enjoy the state of "not" greed. In the Removal of Distracting Thought Sutta, the Buddha presents a series of vivid comparisons that illustrate ways to overcome a negative mental state so that we experience its opposite. The methods are listed in order of increasing forcefulness. If one fails, we try the next.

▸ Replace it: Say that greed, hate, or delusion arises because you pay unwise attention to some aspect of an object. Then pay attention instead to some wholesome aspect, just as a skilled carpenter assembling furniture might tap out a course peg by hammering in a fine one.

▸ Remember the suffering it causes: If the mental state does not go away, examine the danger in it. Contemplate that such thoughts are reprehensible and result in suffering, just as a young man or woman who is fond of ornaments would be horrified, humiliated, and disgusted by the carcass of a snake hung around the neck.

▸ Ignore it: If the thought persists, try to forget it. Pay no attention, just as a man with good eyes who did not want to see something bad would shut his eyes or look away.

▸ Remember that it is impermanent: If the thought still stays, remind yourself that every mental state arises and passes away. Then leaving the first state, the mind goes to the next, just as a man who is walking fast might think, "Why am I walking fast? What if I walk slowly?" Then he walks slowly. Later he might think, "Why am I walking slowly? What if I stand?" Then he stands. Later he might think, "Why am I standing? What if I sit?" Then he sits. Later he might think, "Why am I sitting? What if I lie down?" Then he lies down.

▸ Overpower it: If the thought still remains in your mind, then with teeth clenched and tongue pressed against the roof of your mouth, use all your energy to overcome it. Crush mind with mind, just as a strong man might seize a weaker man by the head or shoulders and beat him down, constrain him, and crush him.

Though negative states of mind are more troublesome and thus require strong measures to overcome them, we should also use mindfulness to encourage states that are wholesome and beneficial. For instance, when thoughts of generosity, loving-friendliness, appreciation, and equanimity arise, we should ask ourselves, "Is my mindfulness strong enough to maintain them? If not, what else can I do?" For instance, we can make changes to our lifestyle, such as living in a suitable place, keeping the house clean, getting together with like-minded friends, reading inspiring books, and developing a diligent daily mindfulness practice.

With mindfulness and effort, we can develop wonderful states of mind, including confidence, patience, concentration, attention, thoughts of service, thoughts of simplicity, determination to good things, thoughts of contentment, and thoughts of wisdom.

KEY POINTS FOR MEDITATION ON MENTAL STATES

▶ To practice mindfulness of mind, begin every day with meditation, using your breath as the primary focus. As the breath becomes calm, subtle, and relaxed, the mind becomes calm and relaxed.

▶ Practice awareness of your mental states by watching them arise, peak, and pass away. Practicing awareness on the cushion helps you to be mindful of mental states in everyday life.

▶ Awareness of impermanence also is impermanent. That is why the mind, while watching mental states arise, peak, and pass away, drifts from this awareness. While you are mindful of the changes of one mental state, another arises. Then leaving the first state, your mind goes to the second. This means that the mind watching impermanence is also changing.

▶ If mindfulness of the impermanence of a harmful mental state is not sufficient to overcome it, try a more forceful method.

▶ When greed, hatred, delusion, and other harmful states are abandoned, the mind is steadied internally and quieted. In this state, it can be brought to singleness and concentrated.

▶ Mindfulness and concentration working together in unison and stability notice countless changes taking place in the mind simultaneously.

▶ Apply mindfulness and attention without concepts. Ideas or thoughts are impediments. Without them, you can focus the mind like a laser beam on the five aggregates. Then the mind can see that *I* exists only when the body, feelings, perceptions, thoughts, and consciousness exist. They, in turn, exist dependent on causes and conditions. They are impermanent. You can't find any self or soul or *I* in any of the aggregates.

▶ Each moment is a new moment. Each moment is a fresh moment. Each moment brings you new insight and new understanding.

▶ Nothing is static. Everything is dynamic. Everything is changing. Everything is appearing and disappearing. Feeling arises and passes away. Thought arises and passes away. Perception arises and passes away. Consciousness arises and passes away. You experience only change.

▶ In the mental state of deep concentration, you see things as they really are.

PART IV:

Mindfulness of Dhamma

10: *Hindrances*

Once when the Venerable Anuruddha was meditating in seclusion, seven thoughts occurred to him. Knowing Anuruddha's thoughts, the Buddha appeared in front of him.

The Blessed One sat down on a prepared seat and said, "Good, Anuruddha, very good. It's good that you think these seven thoughts of a great person: This dhamma is for one who is modest, not one who is boastful; for one who is content, not one who is discontent; for one who is reclusive, not one who is entangled in society. This dhamma is for one who is energetic, not one who is lazy; for one who is mindful, not one who is unmindful; for one whose mind is centered, not one whose mind is distracted; for one who is discerning, not for one who is heedless.

"Now then, Anuruddha, think the eighth thought of a great person: This dhamma is for one who is wise, not for one who delights in delusion." Then the Buddha gave Anuruddha instructions for using his insights to reach states of deep concentration. . . .

Dwelling alone, secluded, heedful, ardent, and resolute, Anuruddha followed the Buddha's instructions and in a short time attained liberation, the supreme goal of the holy life. On becoming one of the arahants, Anuruddha recited this verse:

Knowing my thoughts, the Teacher came to me.
He taught in line with my thoughts, and then further,
Delighting in non-delusion, he taught wisdom.
Knowing his Dhamma, I delighted in doing his bidding.
Knowledge has been obtained; the Buddha's bidding done.

NOW WE COME to the last section of the Four Foundations of Mindfulness Sutta, mindfulness of dhamma. It gives instructions and practical advice to help us overcome things that hold us back from making progress in our meditation. As the story of Anuruddha illustrates, it takes outstanding qualities of mind and heart to reach our spiritual goals. We must be modest, content, reclusive, mindful, centered, discerning, and wise. If we already have these noble qualities, the Dhamma benefits us by leading us toward liberation. If we do not yet have these qualities, the Dhamma helps us to develop them. In practical terms, our mindfulness practice gradually helps us to grow the attributes of enlightenment.

To begin, we remove the habits of mind that block our progress on the path. Our task is like preparing a plot of ground to grow a garden. First, we clear away the brush, weeds, and other obvious obstructions. In the Dhamma, we call these impediments "hindrances." In this chapter, we consider five hindrances and what we can do to remove them.

Once the ground has been cleaned up, at least on the surface, we can begin work at a deeper level. In chapter 11, we dig down to the underlying root system of the hindrances: the five aggregates of clinging, the contact of the senses with sensory objects, and the ten fetters that arise from that contact.

Only when we have uprooted these deep causes can seven positive qualities, called the factors of enlightenment, start to grow. We explore these qualities in chapter 12. Finally, in chapter 13, we look at the Buddha's roadmap of the Dhamma path, the Four Noble Truths and eight mindful steps. It outlines the journey we must take to travel from suffering to freedom.

THE FIVE HINDRANCES

When we practice mindfulness meditation, it doesn't take long for us to discover that it's not always easy to concentrate. Whether we are trying to focus on the breath or to observe the changes in our body, feel-ings, or thoughts, distractions have a way of pulling us off track. The most powerful of these distractions are called the "hindrances." They interfere with our ability to concentrate both during meditation and in everyday life.

We have already mentioned some of the hindrances. For instance, we noted that our *desire* for pleasure and *hatred* for pain hide behind many of our feelings. Other hindrances to progress on the path are *restlessness and worry*, laziness (also called *sloth and torpor*), and *doubt*. Mindfulness helps us to know five important things about the hindrances: when they are present, when they are absent, how they arise, what to do to make them go away, and how to keep them from coming back.

When the hindrances have been overcome, the mind automatically becomes calm, bright, and clear. This clarity is essential to insight into the impermanent, suffering, and selfless nature of everything that exists.

Desire. As a hindrance, desire means more than just "clinging." In Pali, the word used at this point in the Four Foundations of Mindfulness Sutta is *chanda*, which means "willingness to have sense pleasure." As we have noted, the willingness to experience delightful sights, sounds, smells, tastes, and touches often distracts us when we are trying to meditate. As we have all experienced, sense desire also disturbs our concentration at work or when we are trying to finish some household task. How often have we lost focus because we are suddenly hungry for ice cream or because of physical desire for our boyfriend or girl-friend? Distractions like these are chanda, desire for physical pleasure arising from the senses.

Desire can also arise in the sixth sense, the mind. So, while medi-tating, sometimes the sound of a song we like starts running through our mind. Then, instead of paying attention to its arising and vanishing, we want to keep enjoying that sound. If we're not careful, soon our attention is focused on the song rather than on the breath or other meditation subject.

The first step to overcoming the hindrance of desire is recognizing that we have it. So when the wish to see a movie distracts us from our focus, we recognize, "I have this desire in me." Next, rather than feeding our desire by indulging in imaginary enjoyment of it, we use mindfulness to understand its source and suppress it. For instance, we remember that the pleasure that arises from sense contact exists for an instant and disappears just as quickly, leaving us disappointed. We can also reflect about how unattractive or harmful our desire is. For instance, "Ice cream is terrible for me. My face breaks out and it makes me fat!" Or perhaps, "This desire is disrupting my concentration and holding me back from making progress in my meditation. Let me not think of it!"

When the desire is gone, we notice that it is gone. Finally, we use vigilant effort to make sure that it does not return, at least for the remainder of this meditation session. Unfortunately, these measures are only a temporary solution. Until we destroy the roots of desire through deep concentration meditation, it keeps coming back again and again.

Ill will. Ill will includes every kind of aversion from mild irritation to violent hatred. As we have discussed, even ordinary anger makes us feel awful and destroys our ability to concentrate. The story is told about a monk who spent years in solitude meditating in a cave. When he finally emerged and went down to the village, a passerby brushed against him by mistake and stepped on his toe. Immediately the monk cried out in anger, "Get out of my way!" Of course, we have to assume that this unfortunate monk did not meditate correctly using mindfulness and concentration to remove the hindrances and destroy their roots.

The method for overcoming the hindrance of ill will is the same as

we discussed for desire. When irritation arises, we try to notice it immediately so that we can take action to overcome it before it escalates.
The practical suggestions for overcoming anger given on pp. 94–96 are
a good place to start. Keep in mind that every kind of ill will arises from
the wish to be physically separated from something that causes us discomfort or pain. Remember also that ill will and its causes are impermanent. Looking back, we often feel embarrassed that we got angry
over some trivial thing. Over time, like everything else, anger fades
away.

Until it does, we practice patience to keep us from reacting in ways
that we may regret later on. The profound practice of patience calms
the mind and makes us peaceful. Of course, patience does not mean
allowing someone to abuse us. Rather, it is buying time so that our over-
heated emotions cool down and we can respond kindly and appropri-
ately. If ill will arises while we are trying to meditate, we should
remember that anger makes it impossible to think clearly and hinders
our progress on the path.

The most powerful way to get rid of anger is to cultivate the mind
of loving-friendliness, or *metta*. No matter what someone does to make
us angry, we can always find a reason to feel compassion. Perhaps the
person who offended us was sincerely trying to help us, or was physically ill or emotionally disturbed. Metta softens the heart and helps us
to feel sorry for someone who has acted unskillfully. Rather than lashing
out, we think, "How can I help this person?"

When such thoughts have helped us to overcome ill will, we notice
that it is gone. We use mindfulness and diligence to keep this hindrance
from returning.

Sloth and torpor. In everyday life, physical laziness, or sloth, arises for
many reasons. For some, laziness is just a bad habit. For others, it's a
way of escaping from feelings of discontent or depression. When we
have eaten too much rich food, had too much to drink, or exercised too

vigorously, we often feel drowsy. When it becomes a regular occurrence, physical laziness is a problem because we have no drive or energy. It is impossible get any work done. All we want to do is lie down and take a nap.

Mental laziness, or torpor, is an even bigger obstacle to concentration. The mind becomes sluggish and cloudy, like water covered by mossy plants. Everything we try to focus on seems indistinct and very far away. We can't read, we can't think, we can't speak clearly, and even the simplest question is confusing. We have no idea what is happening around us or inside us. This dull state is very close to ignorance, which is sometimes called eternal slumber.

When we meditate, the breath, mind, and body become so relaxed that it's easy to slide into drowsiness or dullness. Although sleepiness is very sweet and we welcome it at the right time, the joys of deep concentration do not arise from laziness. We must not confuse the pleasurable feeling of physical or mental relaxation with the attainment of high meditative states. Insight requires energy, vigor, and sharpness.

When we recognize that we are under the influence of laziness, we pay attention to it. We remember that sloth and torpor hinder our mindfulness and apply remedies to overcome it. For instance, we remember the stories of diligent meditators like Anuruddha who attained liberation by practicing with persistent dedication, not by taking a nap! As Anuruddha realized and the Buddha confirmed, "This dhamma is for the energetic, not for the lazy."

It also helps to talk to our laziness. For instance, we say silently, "I have been born a human being. To be born as a human is rare. The best use of human life is not indulging in the pleasures of dullness and doing nothing. My mind must be clear so that I can free myself from fear, tension, and worry. My ultimate goal is to be free from greed, hatred, and delusion. A lazy person cannot achieve real peace and happiness." In a sutta, an internal pep talk like this is compared to a cowherd who guides cows with a stick. Whenever one of them goes astray, he taps her and makes her come back to the herd. When laziness disappears, we notice that it is gone. We use mindfulness to make sure it does not return.

Here are a few other simple suggestions for overcoming sloth and torpor and for making sure it does not come back:

KEY POINTS FOR OVERCOMING LAZINESS

▶ Open your eyes and roll your eyeballs for a few seconds. Close your eyes and go back to your mindfulness meditation.

▶ Visualize a bright light, a sunny sky, or a dazzling white field of snow. Focus your mind on this image for a few seconds. As you are visualizing, the sleepiness fades away.

▶ Take a deep breath and hold it as long as you can. Then slowly breathe out. Repeat this several times until your body warms up and perspires. Then return to your mindfulness practice.

▶ Stand up and do standing meditation for a few minutes until sleepiness goes away. If it does not, follow the instructions for walking meditation given on pp. 39–40 until sleepiness disappears. Then return to your sitting practice.

▶ Wash your face with cold water. Or pinch your earlobes hard with thumbs and index fingers and really feel the pinch.

▶ Remember the outstanding qualities of the Buddha and allow his example to inspire you.

▶ If sleepiness or dullness occurs frequently, change the time of your meditation session. Some people are most alert in the early morning; others meditate best before bed. Experiment with various times and find one that works best for you.

▶ Consider what other helpful lifestyle changes you might make, such as not eating a meal before you meditate.

▶ If none of these techniques work, practice loving-friendliness for yourself and nap for a few minutes.

Restlessness and worry. This hindrance is the opposite of sloth and torpor. Instead of shutting down and going to sleep, the mind becomes unsettled and hyperactive. It is like water rippled by the wind. We worry about the things that we have not done or have not done properly. We worry about security. We worry that something may go wrong at home, or with our job, or with the family, or with our health, or with the economy. We worry about events in the city, in the country, or on the other side of the world. When this mind gets going, we can always find one thing or another to worry about!

Physical restlessness can also be a problem. We are filled with nervous anxiety and find it impossible to sit still. We pace the floor, pick up the phone and put it down, open the refrigerator even though we're not hungry. We don't know why we are so restless; perhaps there is no reason. Of course, in this state, accomplishing any practical task, let alone sitting down to meditate, are out of the question.

As with the other hindrances, the first step is simply becoming aware that we are restless or worried. We acknowledge that these states make it impossible to concentrate and take action to overcome them. The best remedy is meditation on the breath. As we have noted, when we focus on the breath, our breathing naturally becomes calm. When the breath becomes calm, the mind and body also become calm.

We use the counting technique we have talked about. Breathe in and out. Then count "one." Breathe in and out. Then count "two." Breathe in and out. Then count "three." Go on, counting up to ten. Then do the same, counting down from ten to one. Repeat this cycle, this time counting from one to nine and back down. The third time, count up to eight and back to one. Continue until mind and body settle down.

To keep restlessness and worry from returning, cultivate a feeling of confidence in the Buddha and in his teachings, the path so many people just like us have followed to overcome hindrances and free themselves from suffering.

Doubt. Having doubts is natural. Intelligent doubt—using our own experience and best judgment to make sure that we are on the right course—is actually helpful to progress on the spiritual path. But when doubts take over the mind and prevent us from practicing mindfulness, they are a hindrance. For instance, sometimes we sit down to meditate and immediately start to wonder why we are doing this. We are not sure that the method we are following will work or whether it's the right method for us. We wonder whether we have understood the instructions of our meditation teacher or even if we're the right kind of person for meditation. Once doubt gets going, it gets bigger and bigger. We wonder whether there is any such thing as enlightenment or whether the whole system of meditation makes any sense.

Again, first notice that doubt has arisen. Simply watch until doubt fades away. If it does not, we take stronger measures. Reflect mindfully on the qualities of the Buddha and his Dhamma teachings. Remember other people who have followed these teachings and become inspiring role models. Remember past successes, such as peaceful and focused meditation sessions, times when hindrances such as sleepiness or restlessness were overcome, or other ways we have changed for the better as a result of our practice. Have a talk with doubt. Be gentle but firm. Say, for instance, "Life is short. I cannot allow doubts to keep me from making progress toward my spiritual goals."

When doubt disappears, notice that it is gone. Stay mindful to keep doubt from coming back.

What We Gain

When we overcome the hindrances, even temporarily, it's a great victory. We have cleared the ground, and good qualities—such as faith, effort, mindfulness, concentration, and wisdom—can begin to grow. In a sutta, the Buddha described how good this victory feels:

> Suppose a man with wealth and possessions were traveling along a deserted road where food was scarce and dangers were many. After some time he crossed over the desert and arrived at a village that is safe and free from danger. He would reflect on this, and as a result, he would become glad and experience joy.
>
> In the same way, when a bhikkhu sees that these five hindrances . . . have been abandoned within himself, he regards that as freedom from debt, as good health, as release from prison, as freedom from slavery, as a place of safety. . . . Gladness arises. When he is gladdened, rapture arises. When his mind is filled with rapture, his body becomes tranquil. Tranquil in body, he experiences happiness. Being happy, his mind becomes concentrated.
>
> (tr. Bhikkhu Bodhi)

11: *Clinging and the Fetters*

Once Venerable Sariputta and Venerable Mahakotthita were living in the Deer Park near Varanasi. In the late afternoon, Mahakotthita left his seclusion and went to Sariputta. After exchanging courteous greetings, Mahakotthita said, "Now tell me, friend Sariputta, is the eye the fetter of visible objects, or are visible objects the fetter of the eye? Similarly, is this so for the ear and sounds, the nose and smells, the tongue and tastes, the body and tangible objects, and the mind and mental objects?"

"Friend Kotthita," Sariputta replied, "the eye is not the fetter of visible objects, nor are visible objects the fetter of the eye. Rather, the desire and craving that arise in dependence on both, that is the fetter."

Then Sariputta gave the following example: "Suppose, friend, a black ox and a white ox were yoked together by a single harness. If a man were to say, 'The black ox is the fetter of the white ox, and the white ox is the fetter of the black ox,' would he be speaking rightly?

"No, friend," Sariputta continued. "The black ox is not the fetter of the white ox, nor is the white ox the fetter of the black ox. Rather the single harness by which the two are yoked together, that is the fetter.

"So, too, friend, the eye is not the fetter of visible objects . . . nor are mental objects the fetter of the mind. Rather, the desire and craving that arises in dependence on both, that is the fetter. . . .

"By this line of reasoning, friend," Sariputta concluded, "it may be understood why the Blessed One proclaimed this holy life for the complete destruction of suffering."

"How so?" asked Mahakotthita.

"In this manner," Sariputta replied. "There is an eye in the Blessed One.

The Blessed One sees forms with the eye. Yet there is no desire and craving. Thus it is, also, for the ear, nose, tongue, body, and mind. Because the Blessed One is well liberated in mind, there is the complete destruction of suffering."

(tr. Bhikkhu Bodhi)

....

As we discussed, hindrances are like weeds in a garden. To grow healthy plants, first we must clear away these obvious obstructions. The roots of the hindrances are the fetters. As anyone who has cultivated a garden knows, the root system of a weed is often much larger than the part of the plant above ground. These roots, underlying tendencies in the mind, arise directly from the contact of our senses with sensory objects and consciousness.

As we noted, there are two types of contact, external and internal. An argument with a friend is an example of external contact. As soon as it begins, we think, "*I* am angry. You have said such and such to *me*. You have done this or that with something that is *mine*." Let's call this underlying tendency "I, Me, Mine." It has confused our mind for many lifetimes. "I, Me, Mine" can also arise from internal contact with mental objects, such as the memory of some unkind thing this friend did in the past or the fantasy of what she might do in the future.

Sometimes it feels as if this "I, Me, Mine" exists within the five aggregates of body, feeling, perception, thought, and consciousness. Other times, "I, Me, Mine" seems to be the container of the five aggregates. Or we may think that "I, Me, and Mine" and the aggregates are identical. This fetter—belief in a permanent self—traps us in the cycle of death and rebirth. It causes us to suffer tremendously. Only when this fetter and nine others are uprooted by the special kind of insight known in the Dhamma as "wisdom" can we know without doubt or hesitation that the five aggregates are impermanent, unsatisfactory, and selfless. As Sariputta explained to Mahakotthita, well liberated in mind by wisdom, we attain the complete destruction of suffering.

The Five Aggregates of Clinging

In our ordinary state, the five aggregates are all we know. Eat a meal, take a shower, talk to somebody, listen to something, read a book, and the five aggregates are activated. When we remember the past or imagine the future, we are thinking of the five aggregates. In the present, we sit, stand, walk, talk, eat, drink, and sleep only with the five aggregates.

So which aggregate arises first? It's hard to say because the aggregates are so interlinked. We drink a glass of orange juice. It has citrus acid, citrus oil, vitamin C, sour and sweet taste, orange color, and water. Which of these ingredients do we drink first? The answer is obvious: all of them simultaneously.

However, when we observe our actions carefully, we notice that the intention to do something actually arises first. Intention belongs to the aggregate of thought. But no aggregate works alone. The moment we reach out a hand to pick up the glass, all five aggregates are activated: neurons in brain cells, muscles and tendons, feelings, perceptions, mental energy, contact with some object, and consciousness. If we restrain the hand from picking up the glass, the aggregates linked to the intention to drink the juice stop as well.

As the word "aggregate" reminds us, each of the five aggregates is made up of many parts. Form has many millions of physical particles composed of subatomic particles. Feeling is a collection of 108 kinds of feelings. Feelings arise from contact through the eye, ear, nose, tongue, body, and mind. A feeling can be pleasant, unpleasant, or neutral. It can arise dependent on past experience of contact, present experience of contact, or imagination of future contact. It can be physical or mental. It can be gross or subtle. In the same way, perception, thought, and consciousness arise from various types of contact and have countless minute subdivisions.

So why is this important? Ordinarily, we forget that the aggregates are composed of parts and that these parts are always changing. Moreover, we habitually confuse the aggregates with the fetter we are calling "I, Me, Mine." Since the body is *mine*, we cling to it. We do the same with feelings, perceptions, thoughts, and consciousness. Then they are the "aggregates of clinging." When the aggregates change, as they inevitably do, we suffer. Then they are also the "aggregates of suffering."

The aggregates themselves are neutral. They become aggregates of clinging only when *I* perceive them with *my* senses and make them *my* objects. The difference is our mental state. If we don't cling, the Buddha tells us again and again, we don't suffer. Then they are just the five aggregates—coming into being, existing, and passing away. In a way, we can say that all of the Buddha's teachings are for the purpose of explaining the five aggregates and how to be liberated from them!

Fetters

The source of our confusion is the fetters, deep-rooted habits in the unenlightened mind. Fetters are triggered by contact between the six senses and six sense objects: the eye and visible objects, the ear and sounds, the nose and smells, the tongue and tastes, the body and tangible objects, and the mind and mental objects. As we work with the fetters, we need to keep the example of the white ox and black ox in mind. The fetter is not the eye, nor is it the visible forms that the eye perceives. Rather, fetters arise as a result of contact between the two and consciousness.

When the senses make contact with external objects—a woman walking down the street, a cup of tea, a yellow flower—or internal objects—a memory, thought, idea, or fantasy—pleasant, unpleasant, or neutral feelings arise in the mind, as do thoughts, such as names, ideas, memories, and imagination, and many other conceptions. Because of desire and ignorance, which are also fetters, powerful negative habits lying dormant in the mind come to the forefront of consciousness. A sutta explains the process this way:

Dependent on the eye and forms, eye-consciousness arises. The meeting of the three is contact. With contact as condition, there is feeling. What one feels, that one perceives. What one perceives, one thinks about. What one thinks about, on that, one mentally proliferates. With what one has mentally proliferated about as the source, perceptions and notions born of mental proliferation beset a man with respect to past, future, and present forms cognizable through the eye.

(tr. Bhikkhu Nanamoli and Bhikkhu Bodhi)

This sequence hints at the origin of the whole parade of suffering that makes up a human life. Depending on feeling, craving arises— either to hold on to pleasant feelings or to get away from unpleasant ones. Depending on craving, clinging arises. Depending on clinging, becoming arises. Dependent on becoming, birth arises. And following birth arise growth, decay, death, sorrow, lamentation, pain, grief, and despair!

The good news is that the fetters are not always present. There are many moments in daily life when no fetter has been triggered. When the fetters are absent, we are glad about it. When a fetter arises, we are mindful of it and take steps to overcome it. When it has been overcome, we use mindfulness to protect the mind against fetters that might arise in the future.

Here are the ten fetters. Some of these harmful mental tendencies also arise as hindrances, though there are subtle differences that I will point out as we go along. In general, fetters are embedded more deeply in the mind and are less obvious than hindrances. As a result, it takes more effort and deeper levels of mindfulness and concentration to root them out.

Belief in a permanent self. Earlier, we called this fetter "I, Me, Mine." It commonly appears as the belief that we have a permanent self or soul that was born into this life from a previous one and that will go on to whatever life comes next. It also shows up as the feeling that the person who said or did something yesterday, or last year, or in first grade, is the same person who is reading this book in the present. Mindfulness weakens this fetter. When we experience how often, even within a few minutes, our breath, body, posture, feelings, thoughts, and perceptions change, we begin to see that there is no such thing as a permanent *I*, only a collection of aggregates that are always changing.

Skeptical doubt. As a hindrance, doubt focuses on our practice of mindfulness. We doubt that we're doing it correctly or that it will lead to good results. As a fetter, doubt always refers to the self. We doubt whether the Buddha is correct that there is no such thing as a permanent self or soul. We doubt the principle of kamma. We wonder where the self came from, how it exists in the present, and what will happen to it after death. Healthy doubt is fine because it prompts us to use our intelligence and experience to ponder important questions. But when doubt paralyzes and confuses us, it is harmful and should be abandoned.

Clinging to rituals. In the time of the Buddha, some ascetics stood on one foot until they fell down. Others went naked or rolled in the dust. They did these things because they believed that ritual observances would somehow lead to liberation. Clinging to such beliefs is a fetter. If rituals such as offering incense and flowers to a Buddha image become our main or only practice, and if everybody does that, eventually the Buddha's mindfulness teachings will disappear, and only rituals will remain.

Sensory craving. As a hindrance, desire for sensory pleasure can be suppressed temporarily through deep concentration meditation. But when our meditation ends, desire comes back. That happens because attachment to sensory pleasure is also a fetter that remains latent in the mind. As a fetter, sensory craving traps us in the cycle of suffering lives. One definition of the word "dhamma" is "whatever our minds can remember, imagine, think, create, or produce by way of mental processes." If these phenomena happen to be pleasant, we like them and wish to repeat them, now and in the future. We cherish the pleasant feelings that arise from them so strongly that we even crave rebirth so that we can enjoy them again!

Hatred. The opposite of sensory pleasure is hatred. If we cannot enjoy some pleasure, or if something goes against our wishes, hatred arises in us. For this reason wise people realize that love and hate are two sides of the same coin. Like sensory craving, hatred or ill will can arise as a hindrance during concentration meditation. When we pay attention and reflect properly, it fades away temporarily. However, like desire, the root of hate remains in the mind as a fetter that comes back again and again.

Craving for fine material existence. Craving for fine material existence arises primarily during deep concentration meditation. Because we experience profound peace, we may wish to dwell in that state even after death. Mistakenly, we believe that being reborn in a realm without feeling, perception, thoughts, and consciousness guarantees us permanent happiness. However, even beings born in fine material existence are not exempt from the suffering of death.

Craving for immaterial existence. Similarly, we may mistakenly believe that we can achieve permanent happiness in a realm in which only mind exists. Unfortunately, even subtle immaterial existence comes to an end after many thousands of eons.

Conceit. This fetter arises as the subtle feeling, "This I am." We take pride in our achievements. We are proud of our health, youthful appearance, long life, wealth, family, friends, country, prestige, beauty, power, skill, or strength. Sometimes people are even proud of their spiritual attainments. So long as we have proud thoughts, even very subtle ones, we can never attain full enlightenment.

Restlessness. As a hindrance, restlessness arises because of unfinished business or because of things that we have not done or not done properly. We can overcome it temporarily through deep concentration. As a fetter, restlessness arises in a very subtle way when we are close to attaining enlightenment. We are so tired of everything; we wish to leave the cycle of existence behind. We are restless because we wish to reach enlightenment as quickly as possible.

Ignorance. Ignorance is not knowing the Buddha's teachings, especially the Four Noble Truths. In essence, not recognizing suffering, its cause, its end, and the path leading to that end.

The Ten Perceptions

Cutting through the confusion caused by the fetters takes hard work. In the suttas, the Buddha calls the process "uprooting all conceiving." Through mindfulness and meditation, we train ourselves to regard sense perceptions and the feelings and thoughts that arise from them with a certain detachment.

Detachment from our ordinary way of perceiving comes in stages. We cannot expect to get there all at once. Impermanence is the key. Working with our own experience, we cultivate the awareness that everything is always changing—the six senses, the six objects of the six senses, contact, consciousness, and the feelings and thoughts that arise as a result. Using mindfulness, we replace our ordinary confused way of looking at the world with ten very special perceptions.

Key Points for Mindfulness of the Ten Perceptions

▸ *Perception of impermanence.* You become mindful of impermanence by experiencing it. You ask yourself, "How long have I been reading this book? What changes do I perceive in that time? Are my eyes tired? Is my body uncomfortable? Have I changed my posture? Am I hungry or thirsty? Is my concentration the same as before? Have the ideas in the book changed my mind?" All these and many more are perceptions of impermanence. You do not learn about impermanence from books or teachers or even from the Buddha. You simply pay attention to the changes in your own body and mind.

▸ *Perception of the absence of self.* Perceiving the impermanence of your own aggregates convinces you that nothing within you endures. This perception is not mere imagination. It is your genuine experience. It helps you accept yourself as you are—always changing as a result of causes and conditions. You remember, "What I felt this morning is gone now. What I feel now will not be there tomorrow. Nothing in life gives me permanent self-identity." Perceiving this truth gives you emotional stability.

▸ *Perception of impurities.* When you meditate on the parts of the body, some parts are quite repulsive, for instance bile, phlegm, and pus. You meditate on these impure parts not to make you hate your body or any other body. Rather, you wish to perceive the body realistically. Your aim is clear comprehension and the balanced perception of equanimity. So you meditate on the body until you perceive its parts clearly. Then you apply the same clarity to your perception of feelings, thoughts, perceptions, and consciousness.

▸ *Perception of danger.* Like all human beings, you enjoy pleasure, and pleasure leads to dangerous situations. Divorce, quarrels, greed, jealousy, fear, anxiety, worry, nervous breakdowns—anything can happen because of your attachment to pleasure. Abstaining from pleasure does not free you from danger, but restraining the senses can lessen the danger somewhat. The perception of danger does not mean that you are afraid to get out of bed in the morning. It simply means that you are mindful. When something happens, you are not devastated. You carry on your daily business with awareness.

▸ *Perception of abandoning.* Abandoning is giving up and getting rid of anything unwholesome or unskillful. You think, "I refuse to tolerate the thought of sense desire. I cannot endure the feeling of hatred. I abandon anything that harms me or someone else." The perception of abandoning requires effort. It is not enough simply to perceive what is happening. You must be proactive and nip every wrong feeling or thought in the bud, before it has the chance to bear fruit.

▸ *Perception of dispassion.* Attachment to impermanent things causes suffering. The opposite of attachment is dispassion. Mindful that everything that arises as a result of causes and conditions is impermanent, unsatisfactory, and selfless, you become dispassionate toward everything. You abandon all conceptions. The perception of dispassion arises in a state of calm bliss. Being dispassionate, you gain insight into reality. Insight liberates you from suffering.

▸ *Perception of cessation.* Cessation means "ending." When hindrances such as desire, hatred, and ignorance end as a result of deep concentration meditation, you are free from suffering temporarily. Meditating in this state, you understand: "This is calm; this is excellent. I have given up craving for any kind of rebirth. All conceptions have been extinguished." This very thought of calming all conceptions brings peace and bliss, equal to the peace and bliss of nibbana. You perceive this state of cessation with calmness and tranquility.

▸ *Perception of non-delight in the whole world.* Normally you do everything possible to be delighted in the world. Non-delight sounds awful and rather crazy. But eventually, through deep meditation, you see the impurity of the aggregates, the danger of sense pleasures, and the peace and tranquility of dispassion. Free from hindrances, you become receptive, elated, confident, and ready. You realize, "All that is subject to arising is subject to cessation." Crossing over doubt, you do away with perplexity and gain the courageous perception of non-delight in the whole world.

▸ *Perception of impermanence in all thoughts and conceptions.* When you see that all thoughts and conceptions are impermanent, unsatisfactory, and selfless, you no longer wish to entertain them. You see that rebirth in any form, in any place, brings suffering. You are tired of it all. Your mind is focused on total liberation.

▸ *Perception of breathing in and breathing out.* When you breathe mindfully, you see the arising, existing, and passing away of the form of the breath, or breath-body, immediately as it happens. In the same way, as you breathe in and breathe out, you perceive that feeling, perception, thought, and consciousness are arising, existing, and passing away. When the mind is fully engaged with this "participatory observation," there is no room in the mind for clinging to the aggregates.

Through mindfulness of these perceptions, we eventually realize that the eye, the woman walking down the street, the eye consciousness that arises as a result of contact, the feeling of desire or hatred, and any thoughts, plans, fantasies, and other conceptions that arise in the mind as a result of this perception come into being due to a combination of causes and conditions. They exist for a moment and then pass away. When we see things as they really are, craving diminishes, and we find peace. As the sutta tells us:

> When one abides not inflamed by lust, unfettered, uninfatuated, contemplating danger, then the five aggregates

affected by clinging are diminished for oneself in the future. One's craving . . . is abandoned. One's bodily and mental troubles are abandoned. One's bodily and mental torments are abandoned. One's bodily and mental fevers are abandoned, and one experiences bodily and mental pleasure.

(tr. Bhikkhu Nanamoli and Bhikkhu Bodhi)

12: *Factors of Enlightenment*

Once when the Buddha was living at Rajagaha, the Venerable Mahakassapa, who was living in Pipphali Cave, became very ill. In the evening, the Buddha left his solitude to pay a visit to the Venerable Mahakassapa.

After taking his seat, the Buddha said, "How is it with you, Kassapa? How are you bearing your illness? Are your pains decreasing?"

Mahakassapa replied, "Lord, I am not bearing my illness well. My pain is very great, and it shows no sign of decreasing."

Then the Buddha said, "Kassapa, I have taught seven factors of enlightenment. When these factors are cultivated and carefully developed, they lead to realization and perfect wisdom—in other words, to nibbana.

"What seven?" the Buddha continued. "Mindfulness, investigation into phenomena, energy, joy, tranquility, concentration, and equanimity."

Hearing these words, Kassapa rejoiced. "O Blessed One," he said, "these seven are indeed factors of enlightenment. I welcome the utterance of the Worthy One."

Then and there, Mahakassapa rose from his sickness and his ailment vanished.

T HE SEVEN FACTORS of enlightenment are the qualities we need to achieve the goal of our practice. As our meditation deepens and the fetters subside, these seven positive qualities arise in us. With mindfulness as their crown jewel, the seven factors help us defeat the forces of delusion that disturb our concentration and delay our progress on the path to liberation. The suttas tell a number of stories like that of

Mahakassapa in which even hearing someone speak the names of the factors provides relief from pain, disease, and adversity. Once when the Buddha himself was ill, the Venerable Mahacunda recited the names of the seven factors, and the Buddha's grievous sickness disappeared.

It is easy to memorize the list of the factors of enlightenment, and some people do. But it is not enough just to know what the factors are. We must understanding the meaning of each factor and use our mindfulness to see when it is present, how it arises, and how to develop and maintain it.

In Pali, the seven factors are known as *bojjhangas*. The word comes from *bodhi*, which means "enlightenment," and *anga*, which means "limb." The seven factors we discuss in this chapter are the limbs— the arms and legs of enlightenment. Without them, we cannot walk the path to freedom from suffering. They arise in the same order for everyone. In fact, each marks a stage in our progress along the path. We cannot skip any stage because each develops naturally out of the one before. Let's look more closely at each factor.

MINDFULNESS

Everything we have been discussing so far pertains to mindfulness. All progress on the path starts with this quality. As the Buddha said, "mindfulness is the chief of all the dhammas." But in order for our mindfulness to become a factor leading to enlightenment, it has to be strong, focused, and specific. Here is how the Buddha describes this special kind of mindfulness:

> Bhikkhus, on whatever occasion a bhikkhu abides contemplating the body as a body, ardent, fully aware, and mindful, having put away covetousness and grief for the world—on that occasion unremitting mindfulness is established in him. On whatever occasion unremitting mindfulness is estab-

lished in a bhikkhu—on that occasion the mindfulness enlightenment factor is aroused in him, and he develops it, and by development, it comes to fulfillment in him.

(tr. Bhikkhu Nanamoli and Bhikkhu Bodhi)

What can we learn from these words? First, to become a factor of enlightenment, our mindfulness must have a clear focus, such as the body as a body. We can also focus on feelings, thoughts, or phenomena. These four, of course, are the Four Foundations of Mindfulness we have been considering.

Next, we must be ardent and alert. That means that we meditate with effort and enthusiasm. Third, we must put aside covetousness and grief with reference to the world. In other words, we do not allow feelings and thoughts about ordinary day-to-day concerns to disturb our concentration. Actually, we should put aside greed and distress about the world all the time, not only when we are sitting on the cushion!

Finally, our mindfulness must be unremitting. In other words, we must practice mindfulness all the time, not just while we are meditating. In fact, we should practice mindfulness during all activities, whether we are talking, eating, drinking, or waiting for the bus! Because of mindfulness, even ordinary activities are wholesome and beneficial. If we remember our mindfulness only occasionally, or practice it only during meditation sessions, it will take a very long time to develop to the level necessary to liberate us from the fetters. Mindfulness becomes a factor of enlightenment only when we are fully engaged in being mindful every waking moment.

As we have been discussing, mindfulness requires a specific kind of awareness. In each instant of mindfulness, we are conscious of the changing nature of everything that happens to us. We recognize that none of it can make us permanently happy. Most important, we understand that there is no permanent self or soul who is experiencing any of this.

When mindfulness is established as our constant attitude, we discover that we have been practicing the seven factors of enlightenment all along. When we meditate on mindfulness of the body as a body, we naturally use the factors of investigation, effort, joy, tranquility, concentration, and equanimity. The same is true when we meditate on mindfulness of feelings, thoughts, and phenomena. Our task now is to make our mindfulness even more steady and strong so that mindfulness itself becomes the focus of our meditation. As we continue to meditate in this way, mindfulness becomes a factor of enlightenment and speeds our progress on the path toward liberation.

INVESTIGATION

Wise people are inquisitive. Using our deeply cultivated mindfulness, we investigate the dhammas or phenomena in our own mind and body. Turning inward in this way happens naturally when the mindfulness factor is strong and clear. The focus of our investigation is the five aggregates. Our mindfulness inquires everywhere into our form, feelings, perceptions, thoughts, and consciousness. We see the arising of the breath, postures, clear comprehension, parts of the body, four elements, 108 types of feelings, five hindrances, six senses, and ten fetters that arise depending on the senses and their objects. We see their disappearing nature. We investigate all of them with powerful mindfulness.

How do we investigate? The process is the same for us as it was in the Buddha's time: we listen to the Dhamma, remember what we have heard, and then examine the meaning of the Dhamma we have learned. If anything is unclear or doubt arises, we ask questions, we think, we discuss. We focus our mindfulness on every aspect of our life and activities, on and off the cushion.

For instance, when a thought arises, we investigate to see whether it is spiritually beneficial. We ask, "Does this thought reduce my greed and hatred or increase them? Does it minimize my confusion or add to it? Does it make me, and others, peaceful?" If we discover that the thought increases greed, hatred, and delusion, and destroys peace and happiness, we ask, "What can I do to eliminate it?" If we discover that the thought is wholesome, we ask, "What can I do to maintain it? Is my mindfulness sufficient? If not, how can I improve it?"

We use the same method to investigate the other aggregates. For instance, we inquire into our feelings by asking, "Am I attached to pleasant feelings? Do I reject unpleasant feelings? How many times have I been distracted from my mindfulness by desire for pleasant objects or hatred for unpleasant ones?"

We also investigate how well we understand essential Dhamma concepts, such as impermanence. We ask, "Does it occur to me that the body is mine? What makes me think that it is mine? Do I see that the body's parts and elements are always changing?" Perhaps we discover that our understanding of impermanence is not very clear. We suspect that this confusion may be why the thought that "the body is mine" keeps coming back. As a result, we resolve, "I will spend more time meditating on the body's impermanence."

We also examine our everyday actions and attitudes. We ask, "How many times have I gotten angry when somebody pointed out my faults? How many times have I enjoyed criticizing others? How many times have I taken pleasure in gossiping or quarreling?" If we find that our actions and attitudes are healthy, we investigate how to maintain and strengthen them. If we find that they need to be improved, we figure out what to do to change them.

As we can see from these examples, it is our job to make sure we understand the Four Foundations of Mindfulness and apply this understanding to our meditation and our life. No one can do this hard work for us. We have to manage our own body, mind, and actions every moment of our waking life. No one can walk the path on our behalf. We use mindfulness and intelligent investigation to check whether what we are doing is holding us back or helping us move toward our spiritual goals.

The attitude we should adopt is called "come and see." Nobody has invited us to investigate the Dhamma. There is no place we have to go to engage in this investigation. And there is nothing we can see with our eyes. Rather, the truth of what we experience all the time invites our attention. This truth is called Dhamma. It invites us, saying, "If you want to be free from trouble, look at me." As the sutta tells us, "the Dhamma is directly visible, immediate, inviting one to come and see, to be personally experienced by the wise."

ENERGY

As we continue our investigation of the five aggregates, we become more and more interested in what we are doing. That interest arouses the energy to make even greater effort to stay the course. We experience enthusiasm, along with the determination never to give up. This combination is the energy factor of enlightenment.

A simple example illustrates how investigation arouses energy. When we watch with mindfulness and attention, anything we experience seems to follow a trajectory similar to the motion of a stone thrown into the air. The stone rises as strongly as the power we use to throw it. But as it moves upward, the rising energy reduces, and the speed slows down. Eventually the upward motion stops. Finally the stone reverses course and falls to the ground. Seeing this, we become interested in checking to see whether every instant of feeling, thought, perception, and consciousness follows this pattern. This interest generates the determination to be even more mindful, and the energy factor leading to enlightenment develops within us.

When mindfulness combines with the enlightenment factor of energy, we are increasingly able to use skillful effort to keep from getting caught in greed, hatred, and delusion. Skillful effort helps us distinguish between thoughts and feelings we should welcome and those we must avoid. When harmful impulses arise, we close the doors of our senses to suffocate them. Then we use effort to replace them with beneficial impulses such as generosity, loving-friendliness, and wisdom. Because our energy is aroused, we are not lenient. We do not let down our guard for even an instant. As the sutta tells us, "Realizing that this body is as fragile as a clay pot, and fortifying this mind like a well-defended city, drive out [delusion] with the sword of wisdom."

Until the final battle is won, we use energetic effort to safeguard, secure, and maintain what we have gained. But our energy is calm and focused rather than hyper-intense. Skillful mindfulness, skillful investigation, and skillful effort work together like a well-trained team to purify the mind. We recognize that life is as brief as a flash of lightening, but there is still a chance to liberate ourselves from the cycle of suffering. As the Bodhisatta, the Buddha-to-be, exclaimed with profound determination, "Let my blood dry up, my flesh wither away, my body be reduced to a skeleton; I will not give up what humanly can be attained."

Joy

When the energy factor of enlightenment is strong, joy arises as a factor of deep concentration meditation. The stages of deep concentration meditation, called the *jhanas*, take us "beyond" the ordinary mindfulness that we have been talking about into a series of deeply tranquil, harmonious, and powerful states. As mentioned earlier, I describe the jhana states in detail in my book *Beyond Mindfulness in Plain English*.

As we progress through the successive stages of jhana, the five hindrances are put to sleep and the ten fetters are neutralized, making our concentration even stronger. When the hindrance of ill will is overcome, our meditation becomes joyful. This emotion relaxes the body and mind, generating a feeling of serenity and peace.

As our concentration deepens further, we experience five increasingly intense feelings of joy: minor joy, momentary joy, showering joy, uplifting joy, and all-pervading joy. Minor joy makes our body hair stand on end. Momentary joy is like lightning flashing moment after moment. Showering joy descends on the body and then disappears, like waves breaking on the seashore. Uplifting joy is able to lift the physical body— actually, to move it. A sutta tells the story of a young girl who aroused uplifting joy while contemplating the thought of a shrine. Carried by uplifting joy, the girl traveled to the shrine through the air, arriving before her parents who went there on foot! All-pervading joy suffuses every part of the body.

It's important to keep in mind that the joy we experience in the initial stages of jhana is not the same as the pleasurable feelings of everyday life. And even within the jhana states, the joy that is one of the seven factors of enlightenment arises only as a result of the development of three previous factors—mindfulness, investigation, and energy. Mindfulness combined with investigation shines light into dark areas of the mind. Energy drives our tireless effort to see reality as it is, removing additional obstacles to the attainment of enlightenment.

As obstacles subside, the special kind of joy that is a factor of enlightenment arises in the mind. This joy is more durable than the joy that we experience in the initial stages of jhana. Because it comes from understanding, enlightenment joy never becomes weak or fades. When we reach this state, we remain joyful all the time!

TRANQUILITY

When enlightenment joy is developed and perfected, the factor of tranquility arises. Tranquility is a mental state in which the mind and body are calm, relaxed, and peaceful. There is no part of us that is not steady, still, and tranquil. Desire, grief, and delusion have disappeared. We feel satisfied, safe, and secure. We do not feel like moving the body.

Nor do we feel thirsty, hungry, tired, bored, or lazy. Everything is serene and perfect. Although we have not yet achieved the final goal of our practice, for the moment, we enjoy profound peace and happiness.

CONCENTRATION

In this state of joy and tranquility, concentration becomes noticeably stronger and more focused. In earlier stages of mindfulness meditation, our concentration is unsteady. Moments of clear focus alternate with moments in which we are aware of our internal dialogue and of sounds, smells, and other sense impressions. Increasingly, these distractions fade to the background, and we are able to concentrate exclusively on the breath or other object for longer and longer periods. This improved ability to focus is called "access concentration." It marks the boundary between ordinary meditation and the jhana states of deep concentration.

As we progress through the stages of jhana, concentration becomes a factor of enlightenment. Using concentration as a powerful tool, we focus the mind like a laser beam on the five aggregates. Our concentration penetrates to the three universal characteristics of all conditioned things: the reality of constant change, the unsatisfactory nature of everything that exists, and the complete absence of a permanent self or soul. These characteristics are no longer a theory. We recognize them as essential truths. In jhana, mindfulness and concentration work together to dissolve all barriers to achieving realization.

EQUANIMITY

Equanimity is like the center point on an old-fashioned balance scale. On one side of the scale, we place a heap of rice. On the other side, we place a metal weight. We adjust the quantity of rice until the pointer on the scale is exactly perpendicular. Then we know that we have the correct measurement. This balancing point is equanimity. In the states of jhana, we use equanimity like a balance scale to fine-tune our cultivation of the other enlightenment factors. If we find that the mind is sluggish, we intensify our mindfulness and investigation in order to rouse our energy and restore balance. If the mind is overexcited, we focus on increasing our joy, tranquility, and concentration so that we become more calm.

The equanimity that we experience in the jhana states differs from the type we use in mindfulness meditation to balance harmful and beneficial feelings. Equanimity based on sensual objects—forms, sounds, smell, tastes, and touches—is called "equanimity based on diversity." In the jhana states, the equanimity that arises as a factor of enlightenment is called "equanimity based on unity" because it focuses on a single internal object.

At this late stage of the path, all of the components of the body and mind—the five aggregates in the past, present, and future—are exactly the same. There is no such thing as good, bad, or indifferent. It is all simply reality, impermanent, unsatisfactory, and selfless. In this state of perfect balance, the sutta tells us, "clinging to the material things of the world ceases utterly without remainder."

Key Points for Developing Concentration

The concentration that arises in the jhana states as a factor of enlightenment develops out of the concentration you begin to cultivate the very first time you sit down to meditate. Concentration is like a muscle that strengthens as you exercise it. Here are some ways to build concentration to support every step in your practice of mindfulness:

▶ First make sure that your concentration is wholesome and free of hindrances, such as greed, hatred, and delusion. For instance, concentration motivated by greed for advanced states so that you can travel through the air is not wholesome.

▶ Use skillful effort to put aside feelings and thoughts about ordinary day-to-day concerns. Remind yourself that life is as brief as a flash of lightening. Resolve to use this session of meditation to liberate yourself from the cycle of suffering.

▶ Focus your mind on your chosen object of meditation, such as the breath, postures, parts of the body, four elements, three types of feelings, five hindrances, or ten fetters.

▶ Keep your mind in the present moment. Use unremitting effort to maintain focus on your chosen object. If you find that your mind has wandered from your object, gently but firmly bring it back.

▶ Be ardent and alert. If you find that your mind is sluggish or sleepy, use effort to arouse enthusiasm. If you find that your mind is overexcited or jumpy, focus on your breathing until it calms down.

▶ Be especially alert for any of the five hindrances—desire, hatred, worry, laziness, and doubt. If any hindrance is present, cultivate its opposite. For instance, overcome greed with thoughts of generosity and hatred with thoughts of loving-friendliness. Once the hindrance is gone, refocus the mind on your chosen object.

▶ Your goal is to use concentration as a powerful tool to penetrate to the three universal characteristics of every experience: constant change, the unsatisfactory nature of all conditioned things, and the absence of a permanent self or soul that is aware of any of this.

▶ As your concentration deepens, the mind gradually loses interest in other things and is able to focus on the object of meditation for longer and longer periods.

▶ At this point, you should not investigate the details of your experience. Simply focus mindfully on your chosen object.

▶ Each time you practice wholesome concentration, it is easier to maintain your focus. No matter how briefly you were able to concentrate, you should feel happy about what you have accomplished. Working together as a team, concentration and mindfulness purify the mind and help keep the hindrances suppressed.

► Concentration helps you gain firsthand experience of the truth of the Buddha's message. This motivates you to develop more profound states of concentration so that you can attain deeper insights.

13: *Four Truths and Eight Steps*

After he attained enlightenment, the Buddha reflected on the profound Dhamma truths he had realized. He saw that most beings were so immersed in ignorance that even if he revealed these truths, people might not understand. So he resolved to maintain silence.

But then he thought to himself, "Well, there are some beings with a little dust in their eyes. They are like lotuses in a pond. Some are tiny buds hidden deep in the muddy water. Others are halfway to the surface. Others have emerged from the water, though they are still not ready to bloom. But there are a few that are ready to flower. For their benefit, let me teach the Dhamma."

IN HIS FIRST teaching after attaining enlightenment, delivered at the Deer Park near Varanasi, the Buddha presented what has come to be known as the Four Noble Truths. In his forty-five years of teaching, the Buddha explained these four ideas many times. Mindfulness of them and of the eight steps of the Buddha's path is the key to our own attainment of inner peace and liberation.

So what are these truths? In brief, the first is *suffering*, the dissatisfaction or unhappiness we inevitably feel in our lives. The second is the origin or *cause* of this suffering, our own undisciplined, grasping mind. The third is *cessation*, the truth that by eliminating desire and craving, it is possible to end our suffering. The fourth is the *path*, the eight mindful steps we must take to reach this goal.

Mindfulness of the Four Noble Truths

Many people find it easier to think about other people's problems than about their own. "Look at the state of the world," they say. "It is full of diseases, starvation, joblessness, divorce, war, disasters, and other terrible things." Problems like earthquakes and epidemics seem so real and immediate, it is easy to feel compassion for the victims. Of course, it wonderful to feel moved by the suffering of others and to do what we can to help. But sometimes our concern is a way to forget or ignore the suffering we experience ourselves every day.

The message of the Buddha's *first noble truth* is that every being experiences suffering. Not all suffering is catastrophic. Most is quite ordinary. The Four Foundations of Mindfulness Sutta lists many examples. We suffer because we experience aging, illness, and death. We suffer physically and emotionally because of misfortunes of all kinds. We regularly experience sadness and distress. In essence, we suffer whenever we encounter anything or anyone that is unpleasant or harmful and whenever we are separated from anything or anyone that is pleasant or comforting.

With a moment's reflection, we can all list many personal examples. Whether we call it stress, anxiety, depression, chronic illness, fear, or nervousness, the Buddha's first truth reminds us that in our unenlightened state, suffering is unavoidable.

Mindfulness helps us to recognize that underlying all of these kinds of suffering is desire or clinging. All five aggregates fall sick, grow old, and die every moment. Because we cling to the body, when it ages or becomes ill, we suffer physical pain and emotional distress. Because we wish to hold on to pleasant feelings and to avoid painful ones, life's inevitable ups and downs cause us to feel depressed and unhappy. Every perception of beauty and even the most brilliant or delightful thought arises for an instant and then passes away. If we cling to any aggregate, it becomes an aggregate of clinging—and the cause of suffering. The truth is, it's up to us. When we do not cling, we do not suffer. Mindfulness of this recognition is the *second noble truth*.

However, suffering can end, as the Buddha promised us in his *third noble truth*. As the Buddha has explained, happiness is the peace we experience when our mind is free of negative states—greed, hatred, delusion, birth, growth, decay, death, sorrow, lamentation, pain, grief, and despair. When we give up our thirst for the pleasures of the senses, we stop suffering in its tracks. The eye and sight, the ear and sounds, the nose and smells, the tongue and tastes, the body and touches, and the mind and mental phenomena of all kinds set in motion the train of events that lead to craving and other negative states. But when our mindfulness helps us to recognize that every experience, however delightful or horrible, lasts for only an instant, we short-circuit this process. Suffering ceases, and we remain at peace, knowing reality as it is—impermanent, unsatisfactory, and selfless.

MINDFULNESS OF THE EIGHTFOLD PATH

The *fourth noble truth* is the Buddha's eight-step path. In the Four Foundations of Mindfulness Sutta, the Four Noble Truths are mentioned at the end of the seven factors of enlightenment. This placement makes excellent sense. When we experience the last of the seven factors, the balanced mind of equanimity, we can see our own suffering clearly. We stop getting caught up in the story line. We also see how we cause our suffering and understand that our suffering can end. These realizations are the foundation of our practice of the eight steps of the Buddha's path. The eight steps are easy enough to list, but each is a profound and comprehensive subject that requires an understanding of many related aspects of the Buddha's teachings. I discuss each step in detail in my book *Eight Mindful Steps to Happiness*. In brief, here is the list:

Skillful understanding: We see that every action we take is a cause leading to an effect. We accept that it is up to us to create the causes for the good life we wish to have now and in the future.

Skillful thinking: We cultivate positive thoughts, such as generosity or letting go, loving-friendliness, and compassion.

Skillful speech: We tell the truth and avoid harsh or malicious talk and idle gossip.

Skillful action: We lead moral lives, abstaining from killing, stealing, sexual misconduct, and intoxication.

Skillful livelihood: We choose an ethical profession and conduct ourselves at work with honesty and integrity.

Skillful effort: We are unrelenting in preventing and overcoming negative states of mind and cultivating and maintaining positive states.

Skillful mindfulness: We practice mindfulness meditation daily and cultivate mindfulness as our approach to everyday living.

Skillful concentration: We train our minds in single-pointed focus so that we can attain the jhana states of deep concentration.

Only through diligent practice of these eight steps can we attain the states leading to enlightenment.

THE FRUITS OF THE PATH

As the Four Foundations of Mindfulness Sutta tells us, "if anyone should properly develop these four foundations for seven years . . . or even for seven days, one of two fruits could be expected for that person: either final knowledge here and now or, if there is a trace of clinging left, the state of non-returning." The word "properly" tells us that practicing the Buddha's path requires effort. It is certainly easier to continue our comfortable bad habits. But mindfulness of our own experiences teaches us that as we reduce greed, hatred, and other negative states, we also reduce our dissatisfaction and unhappiness. Mindfulness motivates us to work harder and to strive for the ultimate goal of ending our suffering once and for all.

As our ability to engage in concentration meditation strengthens, we begin to attain the fruits of the path. First, we harmonize the four bases of accomplishment—desire, effort, mind, and investigation. In essence, our desire to end our suffering and the energetic effort we devote to our meditation must be in perfect balance. Our ability to concentrate so that we can investigate phenomena must be neither too tense nor too slack. When these factors are in perfect balance, the mind becomes increasingly open, clear, and luminous, and we develop *iddhipada*, spiritual powers. These help us to destroy the fetters as we progress to higher and higher states.

The path to enlightenment has four concluding stages: stream-enterer, once-returner, non-returner, and arahant. As our practice of the Noble Eightfold Path becomes more and more profound, we progress through these levels of accomplishment.

Stream-enterer. The first milestone we reach is called stream entry.

Once the Buddha said to Venerable Sariputta, "Sariputta, this is said: 'The stream, the stream.' What now, Sariputta, is the stream?"

"This Noble Eightfold Path, venerable sir, is the stream," Sariputta replied.

"Good, good, Sariputta," the Buddha said. "Now, Sariputta, this is said: 'A stream-enterer, a stream-enterer.' What now, Sariputta, is a stream-enterer?"

"One who possesses this Noble Eightfold Path, venerable sir, is called a stream-enterer."

This is an extremely important passage. The Noble Eightfold Path is the "stream we enter" that carries us to enlightenment. When we have meditated for a considerable length of time, our mind gradually becomes clear. Doubts fade away. We see the connection between greed and suffering very clearly. In fact, the two seem almost identical.

Now we practice the Noble Eightfold Path with confirmed confidence. Good morality becomes second nature. We abstain from any destruction of life, from taking what is not given, and from engaging in sexual misconduct. We abandon false speech, divisive speech, harsh speech, and idle gossip. We cultivate positive thoughts and are unrelenting in overcoming negative states of mind and cultivating positive states.

As a result of these good actions of body, speech, and mind, the first three fetters are destroyed—belief in a permanent self, skeptical doubt, and clinging to rituals. We understand that all five aggregates are the same nature, arising and passing away. We have no wish to experience the sorrow of birth, aging, and death ever again. Our only goal is liberation from samsara and freedom from its cycle of suffering. We can honestly declare to ourselves, "I am finished with hell, finished with the animal realm, finished with the domain of ghosts, finished with the plane of misery, the bad destinations, the nether world. I am a stream-enterer, no longer fixed in destiny, with enlightenment as my destination" (tr. Bhikkhu Bodhi).

Once-returner. Next, mindfulness helps us to be more and more aware of each instant of change in the five aggregates. As a result, the most obvious or gross part of the next two fetters, craving for sensory experience and hatred, are destroyed. We become a "once-returner." This term means that we will take rebirth in the human realm at most one more time before we achieve enlightenment.

Non-returner. At the third stage, our deep concentration meditation destroys the remaining subtle aspects of craving and hatred. We become a "non-returner." We will never be reborn in the human realm again. Instead, we will take rebirth in a Pure Abode, which some traditions call a Pure Land. Here we continue our practice toward complete liberation.

Arahant. At the final stage of the path, the five remaining fetters are destroyed by our advanced concentration meditation. We no longer crave rebirth in a fine material realm or an immaterial realm. We overcome conceit and restlessness. The mind is so sharp, clear, and luminous that we can see all Four Noble Truths operating as one unit—suffering, its cause, its end, and the path leading to its end.

Finally, our mind rejects completely the notion that self can be found anywhere in the five aggregates. The last shreds of ignorance of the Four Noble Truths are destroyed, and we become an arahant—one who is completely liberated from suffering. We have achieved the goal of the path. We know, "Birth is finished, the holy life has been led, done is what had to be done, there is nothing further here."

As the Venerable Sariputta explained, "For the arahant, friend, there is nothing further that has to be done and no repetition of what he has already done." The suffering of this life and all future lives is ended, as Sariputta stated: "When these things are developed and cultivated, they lead to a pleasant dwelling in this very life and to mindfulness and clear comprehension."

There is only one doorway to these attainments—dedicated practice of the Four Foundations of Mindfulness.

KEY POINTS FOR PRACTICING THE PATH

▶ The best way to review the main points of the Four Foundations of Mindfulness is to read or recite the short version of the sutta given on pp. 12–14.

- Mindfulness gives you insight into the characteristics of everything that exists: impermanence, dissatisfaction, and selflessness.

- You gain this insight by using mindfulness to investigate your body, feelings, thoughts, and phenomena.

- The best way to begin mindfulness training is to meditate on the breath, as the breath is always present and easy to observe. When the mind is united with the breath, your mind is in the present moment.

- Mindfulness and clear comprehension reveal that the body's thirty-two parts are composed of four elements that are always changing. Because it is subject to growth, decay, disease, and death, the body cannot give you lasting satisfaction. Most important, the body is "not mine, not I, and not my self."

- Mindfulness of feelings helps you become aware that suffering arises from the mind's habitual reactions to three kinds of feelings—craving pleasant feelings, rejecting unpleasant feelings, and experiencing a confused sense of "self" in neutral feelings. Like everything else, feelings arise, peak, and pass away.

- Mindfulness of mind helps you become aware that your thoughts and mental states are also always changing.

- When you cultivate mindfulness of dhammas, or phenomena, you become aware of the arising and disappearing of the five hindrances, ten fetters, five aggregates, six senses and their objects, seven factors of enlightenment, Four Noble Truths, and eights steps of the Buddha's path.

- Properly practicing mindfulness of the Four Foundations leads to nibbana, liberation, complete freedom from suffering. The Buddha has promised that you can achieve this goal within this very life. Proper mindfulness also alleviates suffering right now and makes this life more pleasant.

Glossary

Access Concentration: The improved ability to focus exclusively on the breath or other object for longer and longer periods. It marks the boundary between ordinary meditation and the jhana states of deep concentration.

Aggregates: The five traditional constituents of body and mind: form, feeling, perception, thought, and consciousness.

Arahant: Advanced meditators who have reached the goal of liberation from suffering.

Bhikkhu: A fully ordained monk. A member of the Buddha's sangha, or community of followers.

Bojjhangas: In Pali, the seven factors of enlightenment: mindfulness, investigation, energy, joy, tranquility, concentration, and equanimity. The word comes from *bodhi*, which means "enlightenment" and *anga*, which means limb.

Cessation: Ending. It is the Buddha's third noble truth, the promise that suffering has an end. Cessation with no further rebirth is nibbana, liberation, freedom from suffering.

Delusion: The confused belief in a permanently existing self or soul. We believe that there must be something real and permanent called *I* or *me* that is identical with the body and mind or within the body and mind.

Dependent Arising: Anything that depends for its existence on impermanent and ever-changing causes and conditions. All such things arise, remain for a time, and then disappear.

dhamma (when lowercased): Phenomena. Also the true nature of phenomena, as taught by the Buddha—his profound insight that all conditioned phenomena are impermanent, suffering, and selfless.

Dhamma (capitalized): The teachings of the Buddha.

Dispassion: The opposite of attachment. One of ten special perceptions that arise as a result of mindfulness meditation. Mindful that everything that arises as a result of causes and conditions is impermanent, unsatisfactory, and selfless, you experience dispassion and abandon the belief that attachment to anything in this world can make you permanently happy.

Enlightenment: Full and complete liberation from suffering. By attaining enlightenment, the Buddha and arahants have attained cessation. Having eliminated the fetters that bind someone to the cycle of births and deaths, they will not take rebirth in any form anywhere.

Fetter: The ten deep-rooted habits of the unenlightened mind that bind us to one unsatisfactory life after another.

The Four Noble Truths: The Buddha's first essential teaching, delivered at the Deer Park near Varanasi after he achieved enlightenment: (1) the truth of suffering; (2) the truth of the cause of suffering—craving; (3) the truth of cessation—the end of suffering; and (4) the Noble Eightfold Path—the step-by-step method to ending suffering.

Hindrance: Negative tendencies that obstruct our spiritual progress and interfere with our ability to concentrate. They include sense desire, ill will, sloth and torpor, restlessness and worry, and skeptical doubt. Concentration meditation suppresses the hindrances temporarily, but only the jhana states of concentrated meditation can eliminate them.

Iddhipadda: Spiritual powers that develop as a result of deep concentration meditation. They help us to destroy the fetters and to progress to higher and higher states of accomplishment.

Ignorance: Not knowing the basic insights of the Buddha, especially the Four Noble Truths.

Insight Meditation: Also called vipassana or mindfulness meditation. Focused awareness that helps us gain insight into the nature of the body, feelings, thoughts, and phenomena.

Jhana: The stages of deep concentration meditation that take meditators beyond ordinary mindfulness into a series of deeply tranquil, harmonious, and powerful states.

Kamma: The universal principle of cause and effect. Our countless actions of body, speech, and mind are causes. Our present life and everything that happens to us are the effects that arise from the causes we created in this life or previous lives. In general, good actions lead to good results and bad actions to bad results.

Liberation: Complete freedom from suffering. Nibbana. The state of being free from the cycle of repeated births and deaths in samsara propelled by kamma and craving.

Metta: In Pali, a state of mind characterized by loving-friendliness. In Sanskrit, *maitri*.

Nibbana: The goal of the path—liberation, the extinction of delusion, freedom from the life-after-life cycle of births and deaths. In some Buddhist traditions, "nirvana."

Non-returner: The third level of achievement on the path to liberation. A meditator who reaches this level will never be born in the human realm again. Rebirth will be in a Pure Abode, where practice continues toward complete liberation.

Noble Eightfold Path: The Buddha's fourth noble truth, eight steps to freedom from suffering: skillful understanding, skillful thinking, skillful speech, skillful action, skillful livelihood, skillful effort, skillful mindfulness, and skillful concentration.

Once-Returner: The second level of achievement on the path to liberation. A meditator who reaches this level will take rebirth in the human realm at most one more time before achieving enlightenment.

Pali: The ancient scriptural language of Theravada Buddhism.

Samsara: The life-after-life cycle of birth, illness, aging, and death characterized by suffering.

Sati: "To remember" in Pali. It can also be translated as "mindfulness." Paying direct, non-verbal attention from one moment to the next to what is happening.

Samatha: Concentration meditation. Sometimes translated as "calm abiding." This peaceful, one-pointed mind suppresses the hindrances and makes the mind calm, peaceful, and luminous.

Stream-Enterer: The first milestone on the path to complete liberation characterized by clarity and confidence in the Buddha's Noble Eightfold Path.

Sunnata: Emptiness of self. The wisdom that sees that there is no permanent self or soul and that everything that exists in samsara, including every human being, is impermanent, unsatisfactory, and selfless.

Sutta: Buddhist scripture, especially a narrative or discourse traditionally considered to be delivered by the Buddha or one of his well-known disciples.

Theravada: The Buddhist "tradition of the elders" that practices meditation as a path to nibbana, permanent liberation from suffering. It adheres to the Pali scriptures and is widely practiced in Sri Lanka, Myanmar, Thailand, Laos, and Cambodia, as well as in numerous dhamma centers in the West.

Vipassana: Insight, especially into the true nature of the self and of phenomena. The realization that everything that is conditioned is impermanent, suffering, and selfless.

Index

More Books from Wisdom Publications by Bhante Gunaratana

Mindfulness in Plain English
ISBN 9780861719068 | 224 pages | $14.95 | eBook ISBN 9780861719990

"A masterpiece. I cannot recommend it highly enough."—Jon Kabat-Zinn, author of *Wherever You Go, There You Are*

Eight Mindful Steps to Happiness
Walking the Buddha's Path
ISBN 9780861711765 | 288 pages | $16.95 | eBook ISBN 9780861719204

"Written with the thoroughness and the masterful simplicity so characteristic of his teaching. Bhante Gunaratana presents essential guidelines for turning the Buddha's teachings on the eightfold path into living wisdom."—Larry Rosenberg, author of *Breath by Breath*

Beyond Mindfulness in Plain English
An Introductory Guide to Deeper States of Meditation
ISBN 9780861715299 | 240 pages | $15.95 | eBook ISBN 9780861719952

"*Beyond Mindfulness in Plain English* is succinct and clear, providing the reader with valuable tools to further their practice and to train the mind."—Sharon Salzburg, cofounder of the Insight Meditation Society

Journey to Mindfulness

The Autobiography of Bhante G.

ISBN 9780861713479 | 272 pages | $18.95 | eBook ISBN 9780861718832

"Like the stories of the wisest and kindest of grandfathers. A joy to read."—Sylvia Boorstein, author of *It's Easier Than You Think*

Also Recommended

In the Buddha's Words

An Anthology of Discourses from the Pali Canon

Bhikkhu Bodhi | Foreword by the Dalai Lama

ISBN 9780861714919 | 512 pages | $18.95 | eBook ISBN 9780861719969

Focused and Fearless

A Meditator's Guide to States of Deep Joy, Calm, and Clarity

Shaila Catherine

ISBN 9780861715602 | 280 pages | $17.95 | eBook ISBN 9780861719815

Wisdom Wide and Deep

A Practical Handbook for Mastering Jhana and Vipassana

Shaila Catherine

ISBN 9780861716234 | 576 pages | $22.95 | eBook ISBN 9780861718528

About the Author

Venerable Henepola Gunaratana was ordained at the age of twelve as a Buddhist monk in Malandeniya, Sri Lanka. In 1947, at age twenty, he was given higher ordination in Kandy. He received his education from Vidyasekhara Junior College in Gampaha, Vidyalankara College in Kelaniya, and Buddhist Missionary College in Colombo. Subsequently he traveled to India for five years of missionary work for the Mahabodhi Society, serving the Harijana ("Untouchable") people in Sanchi, Delhi, and Bombay. Later he spent ten years as a missionary in Malaysia, serving as religious advisor to the Sasana Abhivurdhiwardhana Society, the Buddhist Missionary Society, and the Buddhist Youth Federation of Malaysia. He has been a teacher in Kishon Dial School and Temple Road Girls' School and principal of the Buddhist Institute of Kuala Lumpur.

At the invitation of the Sasana Sevaka Society, he came to the United States in 1968 to serve as general secretary of the Buddhist Vihara Society of Washington, D.C. In 1980, he was appointed president of the society. During his years at the Vihara, from 1968 to 1988, he taught courses in Buddhism, conducted meditation retreats, and lectured widely throughout the United States, Canada, Europe, Australia, New Zealand, Africa, and Asia. In addition, from 1973 to 1988 Venerable Gunaratana served as Buddhist chaplain at American University.

He has also pursued his scholarly interests by earning a Ph.D. degree in philosophy from American University. He has taught courses on Buddhism at American University, Georgetown University, and the

University of Maryland. His books and articles have been published in Malaysia, India, Sri Lanka, and the United States. His book *Mindfulness in Plain English* has been translated into many languages and published around the world. An abridged Thai translation has been selected for use in the high school curriculum throughout Thailand.

Since 1982 Venerable Gunaratana has been president of the Bhavana Society, a monastery and retreat center located in the woods of West Virginia (near the Shenandoah Valley), which he cofounded with Matthew Flickstein. Venerable Gunaratana resides at the Bhavana Society, where he ordains and trains monks and nuns, and offers retreats to the general public. He also travels frequently to lecture and lead retreats throughout the world.

In 2000, Venerable Gunaratana received an award for lifetime outstanding achievement from his alma mater, Vidyalankara College.

About Wisdom

WISDOM PUBLICATIONS is dedicated to offering works relating to and inspired by Buddhist traditions.

To learn more about us or to explore our other books, please visit our website at www.wisdompubs.org.

You can subscribe to our e-newsletter or request our print catalog online, or by writing to:

Wisdom Publications
199 Elm Street
Somerville, Massachusetts 02144 USA

You can also contact us at 617-776-7416, or info@wisdompubs.org.

Wisdom is a nonprofit, charitable 501(c)(3) organization and donations in support of our mission are tax deductible.

Wisdom Publications is affiliated with the Foundation for the Preservation of the Mahayana Tradition (FPMT).